LOTUS 2+2s
ELAN, ELITE, ECLAT, EXCEL AND EVORA

MATT YOUNGER |
MIKE YOUNGER

AMBERLEY

First published 2018

Amberley Publishing
The Hill, Stroud,
Gloucestershire, GL5 4EP

www.amberley-books.com

ISBN: 978 1 4456 8253 2 (print)
ISBN: 978 1 4456 8254 9 (ebook)

British Library Cataloguing in Publication Data.
A catalogue record for this book is available from the British Library.

Typeset in 10pt on 13pt Celeste.
Origination by Amberley Publishing.
Printed in the UK.

Contents

Introduction

My first Lotus was a 1979 Elite 503, found for me by my brother, Mike, for the princely sum of £3,000, but unlike so many of the same model today, it was immaculate. In Damask Red with black cloth seats, it was my first taste of Lotus ownership, resulting in sublime driving, lots of admiring looks from passers-by and a huge amount of pride in my new toy. I first saw the Elite in a boys' magazine called *Speed & Power* in 1974, in an article entitled 'A Lotus for the Elite'. The subtle wedge shape and clean lines back to that hatchback rear window were quite eye-catching and new. To my mind it remains unique in its design and is still as striking today as it ever was. The interior looked sporting yet luxurious and well-equipped like my father's Cortina was not! I did try to explain to him how practical an Elite would be, with its rear bucket seats and a cigar lighter! He explained that it cost the same as a decent sized house and that was the end of that line of persuasion. It was surprising in the fact that it boasted four seats and was marketed as a true two-seater sports car, in the 'Grand Tourer' tradition. The other classic description applied to sports cars with four seats, where the rear seats are for occasional use only, is 2+2. Two seats up front, full sized and what you would expect in a sports car, and two seats (or a bench) in the rear for short journeys with adult occupiers or children.

My Lotus Elite in the early nineties.

Years later, when I 'swapped my wife for a Lotus', that Elite, and later an Excel SE, consummated in me a love for the marque, elevating my admiration for what a small sports car company could produce in terms of design and technology and how practical and luxurious a sports car could actually be.

Now, some twenty-four years later, I own three Lotus 2+2 seaters, and though they differ greatly, each is a modern classic in its time and own way and each has Lotus DNA, making it a driving sensation. This book will attempt to chart the development of the 2+2 through Lotus' history, from the Elan +2 of 1967 to the Evora in 2009, and hopefully provide solid, practical advice for any prospective buyers of these models.

Right: My first Lotus Excel, a 1989 SE.

Below: The main Lotus 2+2s to date: (from left to right) Elan +2S, Excel SE and Evora.

1

The Elan +2

Model History

Until the mid-sixties, Lotus was concerned only with the production of racing machinery and two-seater road cars that had excellent handling, styling and verve. However, the market was moving on and the original purchasers of Elans were having families, with the demographic of potential Lotus purchasers moving upmarket, requiring more practicality than the Elan could offer. Colin Chapman, the genius behind Lotus Cars, realised that as his own family was growing, so too were the families of his first generation of Lotus owners. As a result, the company needed to move to match other manufacturers and to provide what the customer base needed – a new model. Indeed, Lotus needed a new direction for the company to follow into the future.

Other manufacturers of sports cars were bringing out 2+2 models and Lotus needed to follow suit. Jaguar had the E-Type, Triumph had the Stag, and even Reliant were producing the Scimitar. Ferrari were producing V12 Gran Turismo two seaters during this period: the 275, the 330, the 365 and 365 Daytona right up to 1974 (and, coincidentally, the end of Elan production for Lotus).

The design process for the first Lotus 2+2 started in 1963 and was based upon extending the existing Elan chassis to accommodate a 2+2 body and extra boot space. It was decided that the final car 'must be capable of transporting two adults and two children 1,000 miles in comfort with their luggage'. It is said that a Team Lotus member was tasked with putting together a working prototype, which was called 'the tub', and this was developed into a second prototype and shown to the Lotus board in 1965 as the Metier II.

The prototype took to the roads in 1965 but was quickly restyled and enlarged, most of the changes being due to Colin Chapman's interventions. Many of these alterations were concerned with the bumpers. The prototype had aluminium bumpers, to move on from the fibreglass items on the original Elan that Chapman didn't care for; however, the complexity of manufacture and the associated cost of these aluminium articles precluded their use on the finished car and existing chrome bumpers were sought, with the front bumper coming from the Ford Anglia while the rear is formed from the ends of the bumper on the Riley Hornet with a section added to increase the width. As development proceeded, 12 inches

The Reliant Scimitar; Princess Anne had one you know.

The Jaguar E-Type, another Elan +2 contemporary.

The Ferrari 250 SWB 1961, a GT contemporary of the Elan +2S.

went on the wheelbase and the track was increased by 7 inches at the front and 6 inches at the rear when compared to the previous Elan. The length of the car went up a full 2 feet and the weight went up by 336 lbs.

The car was also taken to Rover's wind-tunnel and was honed to a claimed .30 drag coefficient (cd), less than the .32 claimed for the Elan. The styling of the Metier bears a passing resemblance to the Rover BRM Le Mans car of the period in having the headlamps inside the wings and the indicators prominent at the front of the wings, sloping backwards, but with the rear taking more from the previous Elite and Elans.

Actual production of the Metier – the name being changed during this period to the Elan +2 – was delayed by Lotus' move to the new factory at Hethel during November 1966, with the first cars actually being produced in September 1967. The Elan +2 was originally to be called the Elite +2, but this was dropped before launch.

The +2 followed the same construction as the original Elan, with the body being made from an upper and a lower section, with an extra moulding that formed the undertray at the front of the car, all bonded together in the mould during manufacturing. This body moulding has a wide central tunnel, under which is the steel backbone chassis, running from a 'Y'-shaped forward section (to accommodate the engine and ancillaries) and a 'T'-shaped rear section (to locate the rear suspension and differential). A development on the +2 was the inclusion of a steel box section beam in each sill, attached to the body by three steel plates and sealed inside the sill for protection from the elements. These beams gave side protection for passengers and added to the rigidity of the body.

This general construction was followed with all Lotus road cars through to the production of the Elise in 1996, the main differences between models depending on which end the engine was located.

The Rover BRM Le Mans car at the National Motor Museum, Gaydon.

Original to the Elan +2S were the front indicators.

The launch car came complete with servo-assisted 10-inch Girling disc brakes all round and Lotus knock-on wheels with Firestone F100 tyres as standard (with Dunlop SP41s or Goodyear G800s as options). The engine was the 118 bhp twin-cam version of the Lotus Cortina engine, driving through a Ford Corsair gearbox. The 3.7:1 rear axle ratio allowed a top speed of 120 mph and provided 0–60 mph in 8.2 seconds. It is worth bearing in mind that the Ford Cortina 1600 was quoted as having a top speed of 86 mph and a 0–60 time of 17 seconds in the same year of manufacture. Even the 1600 GT was only quoted at 13 seconds and 94 mph. Both Cortinas had a 0.95 cd figure and retailed for around £800.

The UK cars used the Weber 40DCOE carburettors but the US export cars were fitted with Zenith Stromberg variable venture carbs, similar to the SU carburettors of the time. This was done to pass US emissions regulations and required a modified cylinder head to accommodate the chokes of the Stromberg units. It also required a bulge on the driver's side of the bonnet to accommodate the extra height of the carburettors.

Knock on wheels on the +2S.

As with all Lotus models, there were an assortment of 'borrowed' parts from other manufacturers: the windscreen is originally from the Ford Capri, raked backwards to add to the sporting look of the car; the heater, steering column, handbrake and internal door fittings are from the Cortina; and the exterior door handles were originally from the Morris 1100/Mini models.

Interestingly, the rear lights on the first 177 Elan +2s were Italian Carrello units borrowed from the Alfa Romeo Giulias of the time, but Lotus quickly changed these to Lucas units, bringing them in line with the Elan S4 and saving money in the process.

The interior featured a polished mahogany dashboard, a push-button radio, electrically operated windows, fully adjustable front seats, safety glass and air horns. There was carpeting throughout as well. The car cost £1,672 in kit form (£373 more than the Elan), but the factory would build the car for £1,923.

As in the previous Elan models the +2 has pop-up headlamps. The original cars' lamps are operated by a vacuum system, against spring pressure, when the valve switch on the dashboard is pulled open. The reservoir for the required vacuum is incorporated into the front cross member of the chassis and the system relies on rubber tubing for its integrity, with two vacuum pods as actuators. Any leaks and the lamps will not pop up! Even healthy +2s and Elans can have eccentric lighting! Later models, from the 130s onwards, were modified to the 'fail-safe' system, where a failure in the vacuum system allowed the lights to rise under spring pressure, thereby guaranteeing the ability to use the headlamps when required. From quite early in production the US cars were given only one vacuum pod and a balance bar that operated both lights at once.

During the summer of 1968, the Elan S4 drop-head coupé was awarded the gold medal in the Coachwork Competition at the London Motor Show and the Elan +2 was given the bronze award. The +2 sold 500 cars more quickly than any previous Lotus model.

Elan door handles were borrowed from many BMC models, including the 1100 and Maxi.

The Elan +2S cabin is sporting luxury.

The Elan +2S dashboard is quite comprehensive and very of its era.

The rear is not exactly spacious but it is well appointed.

The Elan +2S headlamp setup on a 1970 model.

The Elan +2S

In October 1968 the +2S was introduced. The +2 had sold around 1,600 cars and it was time to update the model. The +2S was to be a historical landmark for Lotus as it was the first car that Lotus produced that couldn't be bought in kit form as Chapman went upmarket; build quality was scrutinised and minor details were changed, while the engine remained the same 118 bhp twin-cam unit but from mid-1968 was now built by Lotus at Hethel. Lotus had made the huge move toward being a major motor manufacturer in its own right. The first cars went on sale in March 1969.

Late in 1968 the decision was made to change to the Stromberg carburettors that were used on the US models in order to save money on the more expensive Webers, as well

A +2S of 1969 with steel knock on wheels and the bulge in the bonnet for the Strombergs.

My 1970 Elan +2S without its front grille.

as saving the need to produce two types of cylinder head. These cars also had the bulge in the bonnet to accommodate the higher Strombergs. The Webers were reintroduced in late 1970, however, following customer demand for their return, being more performance orientated.

In a further upmarket move, the interior of the +2 was significantly improved. The dashboard acquired a further two subsidiary dials and the switches proliferated and changed to rocker type rather than 'flick' type. There was also a handy map-reading light underneath the glove box, which was a nice sporting touch! A heated rear windscreen was available, as well as tinted window glass and rear seat belts. The wheels were upgraded to cast items in keeping with the general luxury placement of the car. A workshop manual was also included in the price, which had risen to £2,244.

The map-reading light is a period touch of class.

A nod to the achievements of the Grand Prix team. There are similar badges on the Elite.

The locking petrol-filler cap on the Elan is similar to that carried onto the Elite.

The Elan +2S 130

The profile of the +2S is distinctive and sleek. This example has the Webasto sunroof.

In February 1971, the +2S 130 was introduced. The +2S got the Big Valve engine (126 bhp at 6,500 rpm and 113 lbs of torque at 5,500 rpm). This was the engine that was developed under Tony Rudd, who had joined Lotus from BRM in 1969. He had been responsible for improvements to the twin-cam in the Ford Cortinas and was an ideal addition to Lotus. The inlet valves were enlarged and the ports opened out to improve the engine's breathing, while the compression ratio was raised to 10.3:1 and the Webber 40 DCOE carburettors were re-jetted to compliment the changes. The cam cover was re-designed in black with the 'Big Valve' status declared in raised lettering over the timing chain portion at the front of the engine. The same engine went into the Elan Sprint and the Elan name was dropped from the +2S range.

Later in 1971 the Weber 40s were replaced by their Dellorto equivalents. Dellorto became the carburettors of choice for Lotus for use on their 900 series engines right through to the end of production of these engines in the 1990s. Only the Esprit acquired fuel injection for its 912 engines.

The suspension was largely untouched as it did not require significant upgrading; however, the 'rotoflex' couplings on the driveshafts needed to be stiffened to remove the transmission 'wind-up' that occurred in all of the Elans.

There were also further cosmetic changes, such as a self-coloured roof that appeared on the 130 models. The roof did not require painting during production, having the colour impregnated into the gel-coat on the fibreglass. The +2S performance figures improved to 0–60 mph in 7.7 secs with a 121 mph top speed, which was closely comparable to the Elan Sprint. The coast was £2,626.

The Big Valve engine cam cover – what it says on the tin!

The Big Valve engine with Dellortos fitted.

A late Elan +2S with sparkle roof.

The Elan +2S 130/5

In October 1972 the +2S 130/5 was introduced. The +2S 130 received a five-speed gearbox, which used Austin Maxi cogs and internals in a Lotus-sourced box (with the housing made by Beans Industries), as on the later Elite. This gave more useable performance through the gears and allowed the +2S to keep up with advances among the market competition. The price rose to £2,826.

Production ceased in 1974 and figures on how many +2 variants were produced vary considerably. However, there were between 4,600 and 5,100 cars built altogether, of which only 400 were taxed and on the road in the UK in 2017. A great place to research the history of individual cars and to check on production numbers is www.lotuselan.net, where the original Lotus Elan registry now resides.

The Elite five-speed gearbox with Lotus top plate.

A later Elan +2S Special in black and gold, one of the last in 1973–4.

Lotus Elan +2 (1967–74)

Specification

Engine: Lotus-Ford twin-cam producing 118 bhp at 6,250 rpm.

Gearbox: Four-speed Ford gearbox.

Chassis: Central steel box section backbone with fork extensions front and rear, linked by boxed cross member.

Front Suspension: Pressed steel, unequal-length double wishbones and coil spring/damper units.

Rear Suspension: Strut-type, with tubular lower wishbones and coil spring/damper units.

Wheelbase: 8 ft 0 in.

Front Track: 4 ft 6 in.

Rear Track: 4 ft 7 in.

Overall Length: 14 ft 0 in.

Width: 5 ft 3.5 in.

Weight: 17.5 cwt.

Power: 118 bhp at 6,250 rpm.
0–60 mph: 8.2 seconds.
Max Speed: 121 mph.
Fuel Consumption: 25–28 mpg.

Lotus Elan +2S 130 (1971–72) and 130/5 (1972–74)

Specification
Engine: Lotus-Ford twin-cam 'Big Valve' producing 126 bhp at 6,500 rpm.
Gearbox: Five-speed (Austin Maxi gears in Lotus box).
Chassis: Central steel box section backbone with fork extensions front and rear, linked by boxed cross member.
Front Suspension: Pressed steel, unequal-length double wishbones and coil spring/damper units.
Rear Suspension: Strut-type, with tubular lower wishbones and coil spring/damper units.
Wheelbase: 8 ft 0 in.
Front Track: 4 ft 6 in.
Rear Track: 4 ft 7 in.
Overall Length: 14 ft 0 in.
Width: 5 ft 3.5 in.
Weight: 17.5 cwt.

Performance
Power: 126 bhp at 6,500 rpm
0–60 mph: 7.9 seconds
Max Speed: 124 mph
Fuel Consumption: 25–28 mpg

Buying an Elan +2S

Buying a car of this age and heritage can be a problematic process and is definitely a case of 'buyer beware'. We will cover the main aspects you need to consider if you want to enter into ownership. This cannot be taken as a definitive and complete checklist, but will help you to steer clear of major problems and hopefully imbue any prospective buyer with a lot of pertinent questions and bargaining points. If you look at a car and have specific questions or concerns, try the 'Classic Lotus Elan and Plus 2 Owners' group on Facebook as there are some very knowledgeable owners on there.

Chassis
The chassis can be the immediate deal breaker when looking at an Elan of any type and the +2 is no different in this respect. Finding an original chassis on a car of this age is becoming less likely as the years pass. The chassis was not galvanized and not well protected from the

elements and so most have corroded and been replaced with either another Lotus item or possibly an aftermarket item from the likes of Spyder Cars. This in itself is not a problem if the work has been undertaken by someone who is competent, and if the work has been documented well. Remember, whoever did the chassis replacement has, in fact, rebuilt that car – brakes, drivetrain and suspension as well. You will need documentary assurance that the work was of top quality.

Inspect the chassis for rust and damage, throughout its length. Take special note of the suspension turrets and areas that attract road dirt and trap moisture – nooks and crannies! Under the turrets, in the corners, use a screwdriver to move dirt and probe for integrity. Check that it has been treated with rust proofing but that this does not cover up areas that could be rusting away. Look for bulges and uneven surfaces. The front lateral beam, in front of the engine, is also the vacuum reservoir for the headlamp system, so make sure that it is sound and not flaking away.

Ask about the beams in the sills. Have they been inspected at any time and are there any bills for work in this area? There is not a recognised problem with these but it is always good to know if that level of care has been taken. Look at the seams on these, where they are visible from outside the car. Are the seams in good condition, not flaking or expanded by rusting? Anything you are concerned about, ask the owner.

While you are checking the chassis, have a good look at the suspension arms and springs for corrosion or any deformities. It's always a good idea to have an engineer's metal ruler with you to lay on any metal surfaces you are suspicious of to see if they are true. At this point, if you are not completely impressed with the car's documented history and apparent condition, walk away, or do some serious research on replacement parts and labour costs!

The Elan +2S engine bay, showing the chassis' 'Y' shape to the left and right.

The front nearside suspension of the Elan +2S.

Engine

The Lotus twin-cam is a well proven and generally reliable engine, if it is looked after properly. Regular oil changes, with quality oil, are an absolute must. This should be in the car's history file – don't accept excuses about this!

Look for oil leaks and evidence that these may have been wiped away before your arrival. Look for petrol leaks and water leaks at the same time. These are usually easily cured, depending on what is causing the leak, but would need a consideration in the price paid for the car.

Look for blue smoke from the exhaust at start up and during use of the throttle. This could signal valve stem wear or piston wear in older engines. Take the oil cap off the engine when it is running and look for puffing back through the cap hole. If there is significant air movement this usually means there is blow-back around the piston rings, which could signify a massive engine bill in the offing. If you can check the compression in each cylinder, do so!

There can be problems with corrosion around the water outlet from the engine front cover where the water pump is integral to the cover. Burton Power do a replacement system for the original water pump, but this isn't a cheap solution. Check for any leaks around the large pipe on the driver's side of the engine under the carburettors and if you find evidence of leaks over time you could be looking at buying a new timing cover at over £200, plus removal and refitting of the engine!

Most cars have had their radiators replaced at least once in their lifetime but you can check when this was and check if the car has a retrofitted thermostatic fan fitted. These are a good addition to the reliability and effectiveness of the cooling system.

Ready for action, the distributor is cramped under the carbs.

The Elan +2S twin-cam with later model Dellortos fitted.

The twin-cam engine, showing the water pump outlet in the foreground and oil pump under the distributor opening.

The front timing cover showing how the outlet pipe can corrode where it joins the hose.

Ask if the distributor is original (Lucas 23D) or if it has been replaced with one of the new electronic units. You shouldn't be able to tell from looking at the distributor, but the electronic replacements are a major improvement to reliability and efficiency while not sacrificing the look of authenticity of the twin-cam engine. Should you need information, or just decide to swap the distributor yourself, these can be found at www.accuspark.co.uk/distributors and at Powerspark, whose address is www.simonbbc.com. The choice is yours!

The twin-cam engine reference book is *Lotus Twin Cam Engine* by Miles Wilkins – go no further! This is the book to read if you are contemplating disembowelling your engine and tinkering on a higher level. Miles Wilkins owns Fibreglass Services in Arundel, a major supplier of Lotus and licenced Lotus parts, so if you need something...

If you do need parts for the twin-cam, you can also go to Burton Power (www.burtonpower.com) or Quorn Engine Developments (www.qedmotorsport.co.uk). These are reputable suppliers with loads of knowledge and experience. Some parts are cheaper from one or the other; just do your research and you can save pounds.

A great supplier of basic bolts in dedicated packs is Retro Bolts UK on EBay – absolute lifesavers! They do all of the bolts associated with the older cars, including the twin-cam, as it shares the bottom half of the Ford crossflow engine. Another really good EBay supplier for retro parts, in this case ignition leads, is Mr-Retro-Leads-Plugs, who can also be contacted on afitchett@hotmail.com. He only deals in leads and associated plugs, but he knows his stuff and he supplies in various colours!

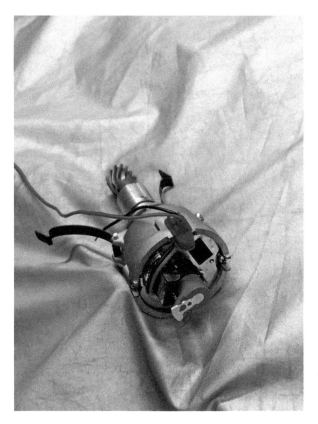

The AccuSpark distributor, showing the magnetic triggerhead replacing points and condenser.

However, do beware! Some long-time suppliers do not always prove to be the most reliable. I have had dealings with one in the Liverpool area who has years of experience and knowledge with another Lotus model sharing common parts with the Elan +2S. He sent me unfinished parts at top prices and became pompous and high-handed when asked if he was paying for their return. A thoroughly unpleasant experience. I would avoid him at all costs! It took nearly a day's work cutting fiberglass and painting to make one of his airboxes an actual working part.

Gearbox and Drivetrain

As explained in the previous section, the gearboxes for the +2S were Ford or Lotus (Maxi in a new casing), and as such getting parts is not as difficult as might have been the case otherwise. These are reasonably reliable and robust units and do not seem to have generic issues.

The driveshaft, however, is the source of one of the biggest issues on the Elans and +2S. In order to cushion the power delivery to the wheels and provide a flexible coupling to accommodate suspension movements at either end of the driveshaft, Lotus used rubber 'Rotoflex' couplings or 'doughnuts' that have six inserts to allow three bolts to be used through each side of the joint. These 'doughnuts' can make the drivetrain feel less than direct and they also have a tendency to perish over time, requiring replacement – in my case, four units at approximately £70 each at the time of publishing. There is an upgrade replacement available from Mick Miller Lotus in Suffolk. The upgrade replaces these units with a completely re-engineered solution – CV joints on new driveshafts that are a direct fit to the Elan. If you are interested in this update, there is a comprehensive discussion and demonstration of their fitting on the episode of *Wheeler Dealers* that features a Lotus Elan. You can also contact Mick Miller Lotus on 01728 603307 or you can see the CV parts on www.mickmillerlotus.com/parts-cv-driveshafts.html.

Interior and Electricals

The seats and trim of most of the +2Ss are of their day – vinyl – although some have leather. Though both are durable materials, after nearly fifty years there will be wear issues with any cars that have not been re-trimmed at some point. The good thing is that there is nothing complex about the seating and the materials for re-covering them are reasonably easy to source.

The dashboard is thin and the varnish can crack around the switches and the edges. This can be removed and refurbished but the number of switches and dials makes this a complex and fiddly job. If you attempt it make sure you have a lot of labels available for all of the wiring and a shed-load of patience.

On the subject of wiring, the +2S does not seem to be as afflicted by the colour-blind wiring technician Lotus employed at one time (making every car unique in its wiring colours regardless of what the manual said!). However, all of the fittings and connectors are period pieces and are subject to corrosion and oxidation, so expect to have to refurbish some of these at some point.

2

The Lotus Elite and Eclat

Model History

For the purposes of this book I consider the Elite to be a 2+2, rather than a true four-seater. This is mainly due to the fact that when you are 6 foot 4 the Elite ceases to be a true four-seater, as no one can get in behind you and you can't get in the back with a normal-sized human in the front seat! I hope this explanation satisfies the purists; it certainly gives me the excuse I need to include one of my favourite Lotus models!

The second incarnation of a Lotus with the name Lotus Elite was launched in May 1974. It carried the Lotus type number M50 and was a successor and step forward from the Elan +2S. Oliver Winterbottom is credited with designing the shape of the Elite and Colin Chapman himself with the overall design of the chassis and suspension for the Elite. This is the last road car that saw any input from Colin Chapman.

The original concept of the Elite M50 is credited to an informal meeting at the factory in 1971. Chapman specified the same type of steel backbone chassis as used in the Elans and +2S previously, but extended and developed for the new car. It is, however, remarkably similar to that of the +2S, with the 'Y' shape of the front expanded to accommodate the 907 engine (and possible 909 V8 engines in the future) and the rear 'T' shape for the mounting of the suspension and transmission components. Particular to the design were rear in-board drum brakes (reputedly from the Ford Transit), situated either side of the Salisbury 7HA differential unit. These would centralise the weight at the rear of the car and compliment another design peculiarity typical of Colin Chapman's philosophy, insomuch that where at all possible every component should have multiple uses to save weight and add efficiency. On the Elite the driveshafts act as the upper link for the suspension, which is an arrangement also found on the Jaguar E-Type and Corvette. The driveshafts themselves are rudimentary units with universal joints, which, as one trained Lotus mechanic once told me, were actually sourced from the steering column of a Scammel truck – though I stress that I have not been able to verify that fact! Unfortunately, this arrangement puts more strain on the driveshafts as the car's suspension deals with bumps in the road, pushing and pulling the shafts, with resulting problems.

The M50 prototype, looking very much like the later M52 Eclat.

The front suspension is independent and follows Lotus, and in particular Colin Chapman's philosophy in providing a reasonable amount of suspension travel with relatively 'soft' springs, but achieving remarkable handling through taut damping and serious attention to the suspension bushes. A GT sports saloon like the Elite needed to handle like every Lotus before it and absorb road imperfections in its stride, which it does admirably. This was achieved by using an upper wishbone, comprising two arms mounted on the chassis with metalastic bushes controlling the movement, the two arms being bolted to an upper ball joint (there was a forged steel upright and a lower trunnion, sourced from Triumph, which was also located with metalastic bushes). This arrangement allowed the bush upon which it rests to aid control of the hub carrier. The lower link is complimented by an anti-roll bar that is located on the front extension of the chassis by two bushes. A very simple arrangement that can also be found in adjusted and developed guises on the Esprit, Eclat and Excel, through to 2002.

The rear suspension, as briefly mentioned previously, adhered to Chapman's philosophy in that the upper link was the driveshaft, saving weight and complication. The lower arrangement comprised a box section fabricated trailing arm located forward on the backbone chassis and a tubular rear link. These were triangulated on their connection to the alloy hub unit. The arrangement ensured the road wheel maintained a constant angle to the road. Coiled springs with the shock absorber inside them (coilovers), mounted at the top on the chassis turret and the bottom on the links fore and aft, complete the setup.

The brakes are fairly conventional in that the front setup comprises solid 10.44 inch by 0.5 inch discs with a conventional Girling opposed calliper that has three pistons – two on the outside of the disc and a larger piston at the rear. This setup is found on all of the Elites and the Eclat, with only the base model Eclat (520) having slightly smaller discs than the Elan +2S and two piston callipers (incidentally, a setup found on the Triumph GT6).

The rear brakes are very conventional (almost outdated) in being 9 inch diameter by 2.25 inch drums with a linkage to operate the handbrake. They are, however, mounted in-board beside the differential, to centralise the weight at the rear of the car and reduce the un-sprung weight of the rear wheels. This lasted until the introduction of the Excel, when the setup became more conventional and used more Toyota components.

The wheels were made by GKN for Lotus and are unique to the Elite and Eclat. Dunlop developed the tyres for the range, providing special 205/60 VR x 14 items that complimented the Elite's suspension setup and weight.

Winterbottom's final design carried the height of the roof over to the end of the passenger compartment, adding headroom for rear seat passengers, and then dropped away with the rear windscreen. This reduced the lift from the rear of the car, which was found in testing of the first incarnations of the Elite.

The Elite has a .30 cd figure – even better than the +2S! The body was produced in much the same way as the previous Lotus road cars, with the bottom and top halves of the structure being bonded at the waistline of the car – quite obviously in this case as there is a plastic trim strip that denotes the boundary. However, the fibreglass is much thicker on this generation of Lotuses, reducing or negating cracking seen in previous models.

The M50 prototype with one of the elegant rear 'tailgates' on the production Elite.

The Elite's rear, with the original wiper arrangement.

As with the +2 there was side impact protection built into the Elite; this time beams were built into the doors, extending from the hinges to the door locks and carrying all of the doors' inner components. These beams helped to carry the weight of the lengthy doors and also provided excellent protection for passengers. Unlike previous Lotus road cars the Elite also incorporated a roll-over hoop that rises through the 'B' pillars and across the roof, again providing passenger cell protection and stiffening the body/chassis.

These additions plus the plastic bumpers that would deform in a crash all went toward the Elite being awarded the Don Safety Award in 1975, which was a true achievement in a lightweight, fibreglass sports car, with the first winner being the Jensen Interceptor FF in 1966 and other notable winners including the Range Rover in 1971!

A further design feature of the Elite that contributes to the integrity and rigidity of the structure is the use of special glass that is thin but high-strength, which is bonded in place on the body. This feature runs right through the Lotus range to the present day.

The Elite is not a true hatchback, however, as there is a bulkhead between the passenger compartment and the boot area, with glazing for rearward vision. Nor is the boot space particularly generous, the original brochure photographs giving an exaggerated impression of the amount of luggage it could hold. The waving adults depicted were about to be sadly disappointed when they tried to fit their four cases into the Elite's boot!

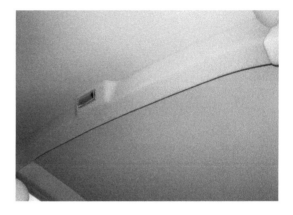

The roll-over hoop in its neat disguise. This is an S2.2 car, so no projector lamp.

The Elite's boot space is not particularly capacious!

Engine

The engine used in the Elite was the Lotus twin-cam, sixteen-valve 907 engine. This engine had been in development since 1966 when Chapman had decided that Lotus needed to be able to produce its own engines and that a 2 litre engine, capable of producing 150 bhp, was what was required for Lotus road cars in the future.

This engine would be canted over at 45 degrees to allow the bonnet to be kept low and it was envisaged that two of these four-cylinder engines could be put together to produce a V8 at some point. This 908/909 type engine never saw production in a Lotus road car due to vibration problems and its thirsty nature – not to mention the development costs that were associated with taking it through to production. The 908 was a race engine and the 909 a road car engine.

The V8 engine that was used in the later Esprits has no lineage from the 900 series engines. At the 1967 Motor Show, Chapman saw the new Vauxhall Victor model, which was equipped with a 2 litre, slant-four engine with almost the exact dimensions of bore and stroke that Lotus were planning to use. The Vauxhall block was cast-iron, not the alloy block planned by Lotus, but it was a relatively easy job to put the Lotus cylinder head on the Vauxhall block and carry out development work. Another development on this engine was the use of a toothed, external belt to drive the camshafts. This was very advanced for the time.

Incidentally, a racing engine, designated type 904, was produced in limited numbers in 1968. It had fuel injection and was used in a type 62 car. A 905 engine, again with an iron block, was used throughout 1968 in a Vauxhall Viva GT and a Bedford van, both owned by

The M50 prototype sporting the 907 engine with polished cam covers, as on the Jensen engines.

The new 907 engine, as installed in the Elite.

Lotus. With 150 bhp on tap, these vehicles no doubt surprised many road users in Norfolk that year. These were the first of the 900 series engines that saw Lotus through the '70s, '80s and '90s in its road cars.

The Elite, Eclat and Excel used two variants of the 900 series engines – the 1,973cc 907 engine and the larger 2,174cc 912 engine. The 907, producing 155 bhp at 6,500 rpm, was an extremely efficient engine for its time, delivering 27 mpg in the Elite and reasonable 0–60 figures of between 7 and 8 seconds. The 907 engined cars have black cam covers that are angled with the cylinder head.

Lotus sold the original 907 engine to Jensen, who were looking for just such a power unit for the Jensen-Healey, a small two-seat sports car they were planning to build. As has been reported widely, the engine was effectively road tested and developed in the Jensen-Healey. The main problems were initially with the oil breathing system, which caused oil to be sucked into the airbox and through the carburettors to be burnt in the engine. This resulted in excessive oil use and needed to be rectified by redesigning the breather system before the engine was used in Lotus' own cars.

Interior

Credited to the Italian designer Giorgetto Giugiaro, the interior of the Elite is quite a luxurious place to be. Most models featured cloth seats with integral headrests, front and rear. Leather could be specified but the seats remained of the same type. The front seats were made to tilt forwards to allow access to the rear, but also reclined and were quite comfortable for their day. The rear seats are of a sculptured design that forces occupants to sit deep in the seat with their knees high in front of them, but they are very comfortable and there is reasonable headroom. I have had friends travel over 100 miles in comfort and remark how surprised they were with the snugness of the arrangement.

The Elite S2.2's rear seating looks very comfortable and still desirable.

All models have a comprehensive dashboard display, with Smiths Instruments dials for the speedometer, rev-counter, oil pressure, water temperature, voltage and fuel level, along with warning lights arranged at the far left and right of the binnacle. The centre of the dashboard is separate from the instrument binnacle and contains an array of push-pull switches (for the panel-lights, for example, and rocker switches for the electric windows and the like). The switches are sourced from the British Leyland parts bin, having their origins with Triumph and Austin, like the indicator and wiper stalks.

The in-car entertainment is also housed in this section and could be specified by the buyer, either radio or cassette-radio, and the centre of console was a clock. The whole dash was trimmed in an artificial wood veneer that might have looked fine in the '70s but looks like it was done using *Blue Peter*'s best 'sticky-backed' plastic, 'Fablon' to anyone else.

Two quirky design touches are the rear-view mirror, perched on the centre section of the dashboard rather than being attached to the screen and the lighting for the centre section of the dash coming from a small projector light mounted on the cover of the anti-roll bar and shining forwards and down onto the area. Great individual touches for a great car.

There were two levels of trim available at launch, the 501 and 502 models, the '50' being the type number of the Elite and the trim levels rising from 1 to 4. The 501 was the base car and the 502 had air conditioning, a better stereo and quartz headlamps. From the outset all cars had a non-galvanised chassis. Lotus used their own patented VARI (Vacuum Assisted Resin Injection) process to produce the bodies, which are much thicker and stronger than previous Lotus models. The VARI process removed the requirement for hand-laying the fibreglass in the moulds and therefore improved the quality of the finish of the final car hugely.

The 503 model was added, this model adding power-assisted steering to the accoutrements of the car. Finally, a 504 model was introduced that brought an automatic gearbox to the mix. The Borg Warner BW65 gearbox was used on the 504 and was available from October 1975.

The interior of the Elite still looks good today.

The S2.2 Elite

Mark Britten's Elite S2.2 – a prime example.

The type M83 Elite (or S2.2) followed in 1980 with a major facelift and the new 912 engine. The 912 engine was developed from the 911 unit used in the Talbot Sunbeam Lotus, using modified cams to improve the power range and flexibility of the engine, as well as many more improvements, and of course a lengthening of the stroke from 69.2 mm to 76.2 mm to give a displacement of 2,174cc. The power of the engine was greatly improved, with torque at 5,000 rpm up from 140 lb ft to 160 lb ft, but with 140 lb ft available from only 2,300 rpm in the new unit. Bhp was also up from 155 bhp to 160 bhp at 6,400 rpm.

The gearbox was also replaced to deal with the increased power output and became a five-speed Getrag unit. Headlamps became electrically raised rather than vacuum devices, a front spoiler and a new rear bumper that incorporated Rover SD1 lights were added and a centrally placed licence plate was also included.

The rear window was given a lockable catch and the wiper was now mounted on the window, and from May onwards the chassis was galvanised. The wheels were also changed for Speedline wheels, which also found their way onto the Excel and the Esprit and brought a distinctly Italian look to the cars.

The S2.2 interior was basically the same as the original car, with changes to the centre console of the dashboard, the deletion of the projection lighting and new colour schemes for the cloth and/or leather.

The Elite S2.2 engine, showing little external difference to the original 907 unit.

A rear view of the Elite S2.2 showing the S2.2 rear bumper with new lights and the central wiper.

The new rear with Rover SD1 lights mounted upside down and the central number plate.

Left: The Elite S2.2's front seats remain the same style as the original and the cabin looks very well made.

Below: The Elite S2.2's dashboard, showing the new layout and newer switchgear.

The Elite was a huge step forward into the executive car market, and with it came huge commitment and intentions. It was the most expensive four-cylinder-engined car in the world at the time, giving it a lot to live up to.

An Elite S2.2 looking every bit the executive sports car.

The Lotus Eclat

An early Eclat, with its chrome mirrors and windscreen wiper.

In October 1975, the Lotus Eclat (Lotus type number M52) was launched. The Eclat was identical to the Elite from the nose to the 'B' pillars, after which the roof line was changed, with a sharper angled slope, and a conventional rear window sloping into the boot lid. The styling change gave a much more sporting look to the car and made it a definite 2+2, with slightly less headroom in the rear seats. Just take a look at the previous pictures of Oliver Winterbottom's original design prototype!

The Eclat used the four-speed Ford Granada gearbox and was issued in 520 model trim at launch. The original Eclat had only 5.5 in. x 13 in. steel wheels, a single exhaust pipe and basic equipment levels. The higher ratio 3.73:1 differential was used to compliment the four-speed gearbox and the whole package was priced at £5,730 – considerably cheaper than the Elite's starting price of £6,483.

In April 1976 the Eclat 521 appeared, with the addition of a 4.1:1 differential ratio and 7-inch-wide wheels. As with the numbering of models on the Elite, the 523 had the addition of power-assisted steering. The 524 model was introduced in February 1976 as the top of the model range, incorporating the Borg Warner BW65 automatic gearbox, as in the Elite.

The Eclat, looking exactly like the Elite back to the rear quarters.

A racing Eclat pictured at Croft. Note the air intake and cut-off poking out of the grill.

In February 1977 the Eclat Sprint became available as an option in the UK. The Sprint was white with black stripes down the lower flanks and up the bonnet and had a black boot lid. There were new 5.5 in. x 13 in. alloys with 185/70 HR 13 tyres and a higher final drive. The specification of the Sprint was based upon the lower 520 model and retained a four-speed gearbox, while 521 Sprint models had the standard 7 in. x 14 in. alloys and the five-speed gearbox.

In April 1980, when the Series 2 Elite was launched with the new version of the 907 engine, the 912 being the main development, there was a Series 2 Eclat as well – the S2.2. There were styling revisions as previously described for the Elite, with a new front spoiler, redesigned sills and Speedline wheels, as well as more luxury for the occupants.

The headlamp lifters became electric, with halogen headlamps fitted as standard. In October 1981 two 'Riviera' models were launched and this signalled the final trim for the Elite and Eclat.

If you are an aficionado of the Elite and haven't seen it already you need to watch *Project M50*, a thirty-minute documentary about the gestation and birth of the Elite that is a must-see!

The Eclat, typically in front of a TVR Griffith and an Alfa Romeo!

Mark Britten's white Eclat S2.2.

A Lotus Eclat Riviera; note the Riviera decals on the rear quarter.

The Eclat Riviera, showing its revised bonnet and sunroof.

The 'Riviera' bonnet, with revised air outlets – a racy improvement.

The 'Riviera' lift-out roof on an Elite.

Mark's white Eclat S2.2, showing its sporting coupé lines.

The Eclat S2.2, showing the new rear bumper and decals.

Lotus Elite 1974–80

Specification 503 Model
Engine: Lotus type 907 of 1,973cc.
Gearbox: Five-speed Lotus casing with Austin Maxi gears.
Chassis: Steel backbone with two prongs at the front linked by box section cross-member.
Front Suspension: Pressed steel double wishbones and coil spring/damper units.
Rear Suspension: Fixed-length driveshafts, radius arms and coil spring/damper units.
Wheelbase: 8 ft 1.8 in.
Front Track: 4 ft 10 in.
Rear Track: 4 ft 11 in.
Overall Length: 14 ft 11 in.
Width: 5 ft 11.5 in.
Unladen Weight: 21.78 cwt.

Lotus Elite 1980–82

Specification: Elite 2.2
Engine: Lotus type 912 of 2,174cc.
Gearbox: Five-speed Getrag gearbox.
Chassis: Steel backbone with two prongs at the front linked by box section cross-member.
Front Suspension: Pressed steel double wishbones and coil spring/damper units.
Rear Suspension: Fixed-length driveshafts, radius arms and coil spring/damper units.
Wheelbase: 8 ft 1.8 in.
Front Track: 4 ft 10 in.
Rear Track: 4 ft 11 in.
Overall Length: 14 ft 11 in.
Width: 5 ft 11.5 in.
Unladen Weight: 21.78 cwt.

Lotus Eclat 1975–82

Specification 503 Model
Engine: Lotus type 907 of 1,973cc.
Gearbox: Austin Maxi gears in Lotus casing. Four-speed Ford gearbox on 'Sprint'.
Chassis: Steel backbone with two prongs at the front linked by box section cross-member.
Front Suspension: Pressed steel double wishbones and coil spring/damper units.
Rear Suspension: Fixed-length driveshafts, lower wishbones, pressed steel semi-trailing radius arms and coil spring/damper units.
Wheelbase: 8 ft 1.8 in.
Front Track: 4 ft 10.5 in.
Rear Track: 4 ft 11 in.
Overall Track: 14 ft 7.5 in.
Width: 5 ft 11.5 in.
Unladen Weight: 23.62 cwt.

Lotus Eclat: 1980–82

Specification S2.2
Engine: Lotus type 912 of 2,174cc.
Gearbox: Getrag five-speed.
Chassis: Steel backbone with two prongs at the front linked by box section cross-member.
Front Suspension: Pressed steel double wishbones and coil spring/damper units.
Rear Suspension: Fixed-length driveshafts, lower wishbones, pressed steel semi-trailing radius arms and coil spring/damper units.
Wheelbase: 8 ft 1.8 in.
Front Track: 4 ft 10.5 in.

Rear Track: 4 ft 11 in.
Overall Length: 14 ft 7.5 in.
Width: 5 ft 11.5 in.
Unladen Weight: 23.62 cwt.

Elite/Eclat Buyer's Guide

This list should be considered as the worst-case scenario. It is not what to expect, it is what to check, just in case! Most cars you will see will have a full Lotus service history and will be beautiful, reliable, exciting and fast! You can then use the list as a preventative maintenance inventory.

Engine

Original 907-engined cars have few troubles. After 70,000 miles you might start looking at bills, though if serviced properly the unit's good for 100,000 miles and I haven't had to have major surgery done on any engine yet.

Make sure the cambelt changes have been done at least every 24,000 miles, more often if stored. Changing a cambelt is not a particularly difficult job, made easier by removing the bonnet first. You will need access to a Borroughs gauge to check the tension on the belt is correct; a local garage may be able to help in this respect.

There are no inherent problems with the engine but it is always a good idea to check oil and water to make sure they haven't decided to join forces somewhere. Also check compression, which should be even across the four cylinders. If it isn't and the middle cylinders are down, it's probably the head gasket – or worse, the head itself. If it has suffered an overheating problem at some time, the head may have warped. That is expensive to fix, if it can be fixed.

Some cars, especially early cars up to 1976, can develop oil leaks through the camshaft oil seals, but this is fairly easily remedied with the engine still in the car. The oil will be visible and easy to trace to the end of the camshafts. The cam covers can weep oil into the spark plug holes, but this is easily fixed with a new gasket, carefully fitted and being careful not to over-tighten the cam covers.

Cars that have stood a while may suffer from 'stuck' piston rings, affecting compression. Try a little (not a lot!) Redex petrol additive or Forte original additive, in the piston bores with the plugs out; turn the engine over a few times and let the additives do their thing overnight. Then try starting the engine up and after the smoke cloud clears, check the compression again. Sometimes a long run, being careful with the throttle, can dislodge the stuck rings.

The Elite and early Eclats can suffer from overheating, due mainly to the airflow through the radiator and the engine bay area. The cooling fan is also inadequate in certain circumstances and has been known to fail. S2 models had improved airflow in this area. Some owners fit double fan units as in the Excel, and more effective, modern thermo-switches. This is definitely something to check while you are looking at and driving the car. Let it reach working temperature and beyond, watch the gauge and wait for the fans to cut in. If they don't cut in at around 90 degrees, they aren't working properly and you may want to run the car through some moving air before it destroys the engine.

The 900 series engine was designed to run on unleaded petrol and does not require expensive mechanical changes to do so. Don't be misled (or mis*lead* even)!

Gearbox and Drivetrain

The original gearbox comprised Austin Maxi cogs and shafts put into a different casing made by Beans Industries and assembled in house at Hethel.

This box is fairly reliable but make sure the lubrication servicing has been kept up, especially if the owner has undertaken this themselves. The front bearing can dry out if not immersed in oil and this leads to weeping oil onto, or past, the clutch and drips from the bell housing. You can listen to the noise with the gearbox in neutral, depressing and releasing the clutch. Grumbling or squealing can be the release bearing or (rumbling especially) the gearbox front bearing; both require inspection and both require the engine out of the car.

The propshaft is usually reliable if lubricated. There are grease nipples on the universal joints for this purpose. The differential is a Salisbury unit and is again generally reliable if lubricated correctly.

The driveshafts are a major weakness. In true Chapman minimalist style, the driveshafts on the Elite double up as the top link of the rear suspension. The shafts unfortunately take more strain than they can handle. As the suspension rises and falls, the pulling and pushing forces in the joints wear them in a direction that they weren't designed to be stressed. The universal joints can wear badly, especially if not greased properly and regularly. The characteristic grumbling is a real giveaway. GKN bearings are recommended. The rear wheel bearings also wear for the same reason, as the pulling and pushing forces load them with directional forces they can't deal with – not surprisingly when you realise the original rear bearings were two Austin Maxi units put together, with a spacer between them. These should be replaced with the later revised bearings to avoid further problems.

The Elite
five-speed gearbox
with Lotus top
plate.

Chassis

Up to May 1980 the chassis is pre-galvanised, and so has to be approached with caution. Nooks and crannies, such as the insides, tops and backs of the spring turret uprights and the parts of the backbone that can be struck by stones, should be checked carefully. The chassis just in front of the rear silencers is particularly prone to corrosion so look for 'botched' repairs. Ideally look for cars that have been given a new chassis, though these are not as common as with the Elans, as renewing a chassis on an Elite is not as positive an economic proposition due to fairly low resale values for the finished car.

The rear crossmember connects the tops of the spring uprights and is hidden in the rear bodywork. It is difficult to see and inspect and has a strip of cushioning material between it and the rear bodywork. This material strip effectively retains moisture and rots the crossmember so it needs checking carefully. If the crossmember fails, the rigidity of the rear of the car is badly compromised, with each spring post being unrestrained and allowed to move in response to forces upon it.

Look for sections that look newer than surrounding areas and for recent painting, unless it is the whole chassis after a restoration. Places that collect mud can be a problem as this retains moisture and stays put, rotting the metal behind it. Make sure you can see the actual metal surfaces. A rubber hammer can come in handy when checking structural rigidity but be careful not to cause damage to someone's car!

Suspension

At the front, carry out the same checks as with the Excel. There are no real problems to look for as this is a tried and tested arrangement. Do the same checks on dampers, trunnions, ball joints and the like. Check the lower trunnions for wear by levering the hub away from the car and seeing if it is loose. The trunnions are not expensive or difficult to replace, but do adversely affect handling if they are slack. Sometimes the locating bolt can be difficult to remove if it has corroded to the sleeve it sits in, but this is not a massive job.

Check for cracking in the lower wishbone where it joins the chassis. The early cars have fabricated lower links and later cars have cast units.

At the rear the long bolts that secure the lower trailing arms have been known to shear in situ and need to be replaced with the Lotus replacement part; these are of aircraft industry tensile strength and no cheaper replacement should be considered. This is usually only a problem on much older cars. Check that the arms have not been 'bodged' or had patches welded in to get rid of corrosion damage. There are plenty of second-hand suspension arms available and they are not difficult to fit, but someone who has botched a repair of this type may have skimped elsewhere and problems may have been concealed. Walk away if you suspect this kind of work has been done.

Steering

The steering column runs into a double universal joint just past the bulkhead, into the engine bay and behind the driver's side front wheel arch. This joint is exposed and can become covered in road dirt, eventually resulting in wear, which shows up clearly in the steering. If the car has stood for a good length of time and the steering is heavy, check this joint as it may just need lubricating and freeing. Remember that on cars without power steering these joints take a lot of strain at parking speeds and that is when any wear can be most easily detected.

Brakes

Generally reliable and cheap to replace. The back in-board drums are reputedly from a Ford Transit or Cortina 3.0 litre, or probably both! There was a tendency in early cars for the differential unit to dump its hydraulic contents into the rear drums through the bearing seals (originally due to loads from the driveshafts), though this has usually been sorted out during normal servicing and updates. It is still worth a check, as servicing the rear brakes is a tricky affair. Check the wheel bearings, particularly those on the driveshaft side.

Bodywork

In cars that have been stored in damp conditions, the paint can start to 'bleb', with lots of tiny bubbles appearing between the gel coat and the paint. This is usually caused by moisture ingress through the fibreglass panel due to failure (or substandard preparation) of the gel coat. The rear of the panel might even be the cause of the problem, with moisture finding its way through the panel and the substandard gel coat. If the offending area is dried out immediately the damage can be minimised, but generally if this has happened the paintwork is ruined.

The rear wiper on the S1 Elite has a clever wheel and cam arrangement to lift the wiper arm clear of the window when parking. The problem is that the small wheel corrodes and falls off. The wiper no longer parks correctly away from the window glass and inhibits the opening of the window.

The chromed embellishments to the window surrounds and roof are very fragile and easily damaged, so check these carefully. They will have been removed if the car has been re-sprayed and they can be ill-fitting and distorted if refitted without absolute care. These parts are very difficult to source.

The body joint cover that runs around the car's waist can become detached, especially if the car has been damaged in an accident or bumped slightly. The strips are cheap and reasonably easily replaced but their omission is a source of concern and should be investigated.

Mark Britten's Elite S2, showing off its Speedline wheels and S2 front spoiler.

Look for contact damage to the plastic bumpers as these are easily damaged. The 'pads' on the later Excel bumpers are very scarce and difficult to fit as they would require the removal of the bumper assembly, and in our experience the main bolt for the bumper is always seized.

Interior
Fabric seats can suffer badly from wear. They are reasonably easily re-upholstered but can be an indicator of general care and maintenance. They lose shape as the foam padding decays and becomes powdery, and can need a lot of work. Switches are all from other manufacturers' parts bins, as are the indicator/wiper stalks, so check scrap yards and Austin, Morris and British Leyland breakers and suppliers before you look anywhere else.

Electrics
The headlamp lifters are not in themselves electrically operated; the valves that control lowering and raising of the units are, however. These are a weak spot, as are the tubes from the vacuum pods. Leaks cause the headlamps to stay open all the time or creep open when the engine is off, which is a carry-over from the Elan era failsafe system. Switches are generally Austin Princess and British Leyland parts.

Wheels and Tyres
The original alloy wheels need to be polished and protected on a regular basis but otherwise there are no other problems to report, other than checking for kerbing, as usual! See advice on tyres in the Elan +2S section as it also applies here.

Exhaust
The exhaust poses no real exceptional problems. It is hung from rubber rings that can stretch, perish and snap over time, so check their condition and for corrosion. After-market systems can be difficult to fit around the suspension and driveshafts so check they are fitted correctly or you'll hear the knocking straight away. A good tip is to take plenty of pictures before removing an original system to give yourself a reference point when fitting the new parts.

Miscellaneous
Water leaks from the front, through the cabin front bulkhead, and sometimes from the rear screens, are quite common on earlier cars. The front leaks are usually due to dislodged grommets or leaks around fittings and can be very easily remedied with modern sealants. These leaks can cause problems with the electrics as the main fuse box is in the front. The petrol pump can also suffer as it is mounted low in the boot, and can be immersed if water is allowed to pool in that area.

The other place a leak can develop is through the door seals onto the window glass, especially where the seal negotiates the upright for the quarter glass. This can allow water to drip down through the doors and into the interior of the car. This can also cause electrical problems with the windows and wing mirrors. Check for water in the footwells and evidence of moisture in general.

3

The Lotus Excel

Model History

In 1982 the Eclat Excel was launched. Developed from the Eclat, the Eclat Excel was what the car was named at its inception and as it showed up on owners' V5 documents throughout the production of the Excel. This was more than a facelift model. Lotus Cars was in the doldrums in 1981, with problems in production numbers (down to a mere 381 cars), profits at less than £500,000 and the Lotus 88 about to be outlawed by the Formula One legislators. There had been better days at Hethel.

Lotus found itself without the necessary funds to develop outright new models and therefore looked to developing the existing models. Colin Chapman came to an agreement with Toyota after Lotus Engineering had worked on the Supra for Toyota and the Japanese firm took a 35 per cent stake in Lotus, which opened up a new supply of automotive parts for Lotus to exploit on their new models. The first model to benefit from the arrangement

The Excel with its original spoiler and lights up, showing the black headlamp surrounds replacing chrome items.

was the Eclat. The Eclat Excel signalled a total revision of the car with Toyota parts and revised brakes, interiors, electrics and rear suspension. A thorough re-working of the chassis, along with a restyled body and as much Toyota running gear as possible, turned the car into an Excel. The model was launched at the NEC Show in October 1982.

Major developments from the Eclat included the Toyota Supra W58 five-speed gearbox and Toyota final drive, which have proved to be extremely reliable and quiet compared to the previous units. The bell housing for the gearbox was manufactured by Lotus to suit the 912 engine fittings. The chassis was galvanised and the rear hubs were modified to incorporate an upper link for the suspension, removing the previous problem with the driveshafts and further improving the handling.

The rear of the Excel with inverted Rover SD1 lights and original lettering.

Rear suspension on the Excel SE, showing the top link and driveshaft.

The clutch was made hydraulic using Toyota parts – a major improvement on the cable-operated system.

The suspension was updated with transverse top links for sideways location and wider, lower wishbones. The driveshafts were also from the Supra and had plunging CV joints, rather than the previous fixed-length articles. Brakes were from the Toyota Celica and the rear discs were mounted out-board for the first time. The discs were ventilated and the handbrake was operated from inside a drum built into the rear discs. Initially, power steering was an option. The first Excels were also produced with Toyota Celica 7 in. x 14 in. alloy wheels, as shown on the sales brochure, before being replaced with Speedline 'Spidersweb' items that really improved the styling.

The cabin looked much the same, although the covering materials were modernised and the rear seats provided an extra 1.5 inches of headroom. Much of the switchgear became Toyota-sourced, and therefore much more reliable and 'sorted'. The dashboard dials were no longer Smiths instruments; VDO instruments were now arranged in a slightly different manner in order to improve visibility through the steering wheel.

The door handles are also Toyota items from the Supra, even though they look like the previous British Leyland items used on the Eclat and Elite. They are a weakness of the Excel models as they are plastic items and have to open quite large and heavy doors (*see the buyer's guide*). The chrome-effect metal finishers of the Elite and Eclat were ditched for a much cleaner, conventional look.

The price was £13,787, a reduction of £1,109 on the outgoing Eclat, and that had been reduced from £16,262! The order books showed 80 per cent of production comprising Excels and things started to look up. Then, tragically, Colin Chapman died on 16 December 1982 and the firm was left without a chairman.

The Excel bonnet with its ventilation slats on the outer areas.

The Excel with its original door mirrors and B pillar covers, new door handles, Speedline wheels from the Eclat S2.2.

The original small but stylish spoiler.

The next major revision of the Excel happened in 1984 with the introduction of the SE (Special Equipment) model. The body got revisions by Peter Stevens; the bib spoiler was added to the front along with two different boot spoilers – a larger, more raised item for the SE, and a smaller, lower version on the ordinary model. The interior was revised with a new swept dashboard with wood veneer on the SE models. The wider wheel arches really set the car as it should have been, with a more aggressive and purposeful stance, keeping pace with the Porsche 944, its main competition. It retained the same engine (912) but didn't get what it needed – fuel injection.

The SE engine acquired red, curved profile cam covers and the cam shafts used in the Talbot Sunbeam engine to lengthen the valve opening times, helping engine breathing and therefore power delivery. There was a redesign of the inlet and exhaust ports to improve efficiency, though the valves themselves remained the same size. New cast alloy

Excel with Speedline Spidersweb alloys, rear arch bulges and revised spoiler.

The Excel SE's cloth interior – a very comfortable place to be!

The Excel SE's dashboard, with dials for oil pressure, water temperature, battery and fuel.

cylinder liners, coated in Nikasil – a layer of microscopic silica crystals said to improve wear characteristics – were adopted as well as new Mahle pistons that increased the compression ratio from 9.44:1 to 10.9:1. The carburettors were also uprated to DHLA 45Ds, which feature a third 'power' jet circuit and add to the increased breathing of the engine.

Power increased to 180 bhp at a lower 5,600 rpm and torque up to 165 lb ft at 5,500 rpm. These figures remained the same until the end of production of the Excel.

The wheels on the SE became 7 x 15 Speedline alloys, shod with 215/50 Goodyear Eagle tyres. The 0–60 figure came down from 7.1 seconds to 6.7 seconds and the top speed was raised by 1 mph to 131 mph.

Then, in 1986, General Motors took over Lotus, with a 91 per cent holding, and Toyota relinquished their shares in Lotus at this time. An automatic version of the Excel was the only other addition to the model range in 1987, with the model being designated the SA. It had the Toyota four-speed automatic transmission and the 2.2 180 bhp engine.

In 1989 the final revision of the Excel took place. The ventilation slats moved from the outside of the bonnet back to where the original slats on the Elite were – centrally placed and on the front edge. The front spoiler became deeper and mirrored the spoiler fitted to the Esprit. The SE had a very low rubber lip under the front spoiler and a fibreglass undertray to guide airflow from the radiators under the car.

The rear spoiler was revised, looking more curved and efficient, and the 'spats' behind the rear wheels were retained. The wheels were sourced from Route OZ and were the same style as those on the Stevens Esprit.

By now power steering was standard on the SE and a leather-trimmed Momo steering wheel graced the dash. The tyres became 215/50 x 15, so were slightly larger than the 205/50s on the usual Excel.

The engine was the HC Turbo unit from the Esprit, without the turbo, but with revised cams as in the rally engines used in the Talbot Sunbeam Lotus (911 engine). Power was increased to 180 bhp.

The Excel SE's engine from the carburettor side, showing distributor and carburettors.

Speedline alloys, as on the S2.2 Elite and Eclat.

My Celebration Excel, showing detail changes to the post-1989 cars, including yellow badges on B pillars, as well as on the wheel centres.

My Celebration Excel SE from 1992, showing late model badging on the rear and the late SE spoiler.

The late model 1992 Excel SE dashboard.

The 912 engine in the Excel SE, with rounded cam covers and a red finish.

The rear wheel arches received spats and new spring and damper rates were applied. The traditional yellow badge returned to the bonnet, and usually the wheel hubs. Badging was silver and raised, though there was no 'SE' added. The door mirrors are the same units used by Lamborghini, TVR, Citroen and so many other cars, having heated, electrically adjusted glass.

In 1992 Lotus were sold by GM, who were having worldwide financial problems, and the Excel was discontinued while Lotus contemplated possible ruin.

Lotus Excel

Specification 1982
Engine: Lotus type 912 of 2,174cc.
Gearbox: Toyota AW58 five-speed all-synchromesh.
Chassis: Steel backbone with two prongs at the front linked by box section cross-member.
Front Suspension: Pressed steel double wishbones and coil spring/damper units.
Rear Suspension: Upper links, lower wishbones and coil spring/damper units.
Wheelbase: 8 ft 1.8 in.
Front Track: 4 ft 9.5 in.
Rear Track: 4 ft 9.5 in.
Overall Length: 14 ft 4.3 in.
Width: 5 ft 11.5 in.
Unladen Weight: 22.35 cwt.

Excel 1982–89

Performance
Power: 160 bhp at 6,500 rpm.
0–60 mph: 7.1 seconds.
Max Speed: 130 mph.
Overall Fuel Consumption: 19.5 mpg (28 mpg Government Figures).

Excel SE 1986–90

Performance
Power: 180 bhp at 6,500 rpm.
165 lb ft at 5,500 rpm.
0–60 mph: 6.7 seconds.
Max Speed: 134 mph.
Overall Fuel Consumption: 18.5 mpg (28 mpg Government Figures).

Excel Buyer's Guide

This is a slightly different list of tips as the Excel is quite a bit different to the earlier models. As before, this is not a list of what to expect, just what to check! Most cars will have a full service history and be good to go – you can then use the list as a preventative maintenance inventory.

Chassis
The chassis on the Excel is galvanised and seems to be very durable and rust resistant. Other than in instances where there has been some kind of damage to the galvanising layer, there are not really any issues with this area.

The Excel engine bay; you can see the front cross-member and the 'Y' shape of the chassis as it cradles the engine. This is larger than the +2S arrangement.

Engine

Original 907-engined cars have few troubles; see the tips for the Elite and Eclat.

Cambelts should have been changed regularly, 24,000 miles being about normal, but as these cars do not always cover normal mileages, the belt should be changed every three to five years if the car has been stored more than driven. Oil pressure should be checked although even a perfectly good engine may show a low, but acceptable, pressure when hot.

Right: The Excel SE engine with the air conditioning pump (left) and power steering pump (right) showing.

Below: The Excel SE engine and gearbox, showing the exhaust manifold.

The Excel SE engine in the car.

Gearbox and Drivetrain

The gearbox is a gem. We don't know of anyone ever having trouble with one and dealers laugh if you ask for the price of a replacement. The same is true of the Toyota final drive; I was told that Lotus still have twelve sitting on a shelf in their parts department! Just make sure the oil level is where it should be.

The driveshafts are also very reliable and should last extremely well. The propshaft can be the only weak link if neglected. The joints should be greased and looked after in servicing and then there's no problem. Listen for clunks when you let the clutch in to pull away and make sure there is no rumbling and vibration above 50 mph. There really shouldn't be! There can be some rumbling from the rear of the Excel but it is more likely to be the mountings on the differential becoming hardened, conducting transmission vibration to the chassis.

Suspension

Have a look at the lower rear wishbones as this is the only place where we have heard of corrosion being even a possibility. The springs last very well; even cars with 100,000 miles have the originals still in place and doing well.

The Excel SE rear suspension, showing the spring position behind the hub.

The Excel SE front suspension, showing the upper wishbone and anti-roll bar on the left.

Front dampers tend to be the weak spot. You can check by bouncing the front of the car up and down. If the bounce feels controlled and the spring returns to the normal ride height without further bounces then the dampers are probably okay. If the car bounces easily and feels 'spongy' then the dampers aren't doing their job properly. You will be able to tell on the road if you throw the car left and right quickly at low speed and it feels anything but sure and tight to the road. Excessive roll means something is aging – springs, dampers or anti-roll bar bushes. The original dampers for the Excel range are no longer available so owners have been fitting aftermarket adjustable items and tuning the characteristics themselves. Check if this has been the case and what shock absorbers have been fitted. You might want to re-adjust them to your own preferences if you buy the car, so find out how adjustments are done.

Knocks and groans are to be investigated as a well-sorted Excel doesn't have any. They may only be attributed to worn bushes, which again last very well, but they can be expensive to replace (depending on who does the job, as the bushes themselves are relatively cheap). Let the vendor sort it out!

There was a recall in 1991 on Excel VIN Nos 1612 to 3048 (last four digits). These cars were built from 1984 until September 1990 and had a two-bolt anti-roll bar fastening, not a one-bolt assembly as in previous cars. This is covered by bulletin 1990/1R (Lotus Cars) and you should check that the required work has been carried out.

Steering

This is the same as the Elite/Eclat section, as the steering column joints are the same items. Since the Excel has powered steering there are not many problems with the steering system. Check the gaiters on the steering rack for rips and splits, as the replacement Lotus part is difficult to fit to the rack. The one I bought did not fit the rack.

The steering on the Excel is one of its massive strengths, being light and precise with no vagueness at all. You should be able to drive through most bends as if you are thinking the car through the curves and using your wrists to steer, rather than your arms – it isn't that type of car! If you drive a car where this is not the case, investigate thoroughly.

Brakes

These are fine if they see servicing at reasonable intervals. Try them out on the road; they should have plenty of 'feel' and pull the car up in a straight line. There are replacement seal kits, but if the seals have perished and allowed the water onto the ends of the pistons for any length of time then a new piston – or, more easily, a new calliper – is the likely remedy. Try Classicar Automotive for the callipers, as they do excellent reconditioned items at reasonable prices.

Discs last well and are cheap enough to replace. Upgraded discs are also available and find favour with some discerning owners. Keep inspecting the back surface of the discs, as cars that have stood in garages for a while tend to have damaged rear faces, with moisture having caused corrosion, which then turns into furrows on the disc when the car is used again. This is usually worse on the rear discs as they don't have as much work to do in normal use.

The 1987 Excel SE's ventilation slats on the sides of the bonnet, with the Route Oz wheels and bulging wheel arches also on view.

Bodywork

These cars aren't susceptible to the 'crazing' and 'cracking' problems of the early Lotus models. The fibreglass/composite body will only usually crack if it has been hit with something, and don't let anyone tell you otherwise if you are looking at something they are selling! There are weak spots on used Excels, however. Like all Lotus models, we know that the low nose takes the brunt of stone chips. Excels seem to attract stones like a magnet attracts pins – possibly because they are driven in more daily conditions than most models. The front fog lamps can crack easily; they are about £50 to £70 each to replace, so cover the lens with a layer of sticky transparent plastic as it may help to deflect most stones and you may save the lenses.

The paintwork is generally good, but give it real air and sun, as the car was intended, and the paint can go 'flat' after about ten years on the road. The lacquer layer can 'lift' from the base coat in places on metallic painted cars. Look at the bottom of the windscreen and front edges of the doors for possible problems. The bonnet is most likely to go flat first so look hard here and on the roof for patches that look like the paint has lost its gloss. Position yourself where you can see the light glancing off the panels, rather than the colour of the paint, and check that the car hasn't been badly painted. You shouldn't be able to see swirls or brush-type marks, or patches under the paint. This is a cheap re-spray by someone who doesn't know about fibreglass and has probably rubbed the car down and gone too far, breaching the gel coat on top of the fibreglass; then, when the car is painted, the exposed fibreglass is more porous than the surrounding gel coat and it absorbs the paint, giving an uneven, glossy but 'painted with a brush' look.

The doors are a prominent area of weakness. The handles that replaced the Morris Marina parts on the Eclat and Elite are from Toyota's parts bin (Supra II), but they are plastic and they break. The small bolt that tightens the whole unit to the door can break the plastic when the door handle is pulled too hard and the rear of the handle assembly lifts from the door when the handle is pulled. These are about £50 each to replace so look to make sure someone hasn't already glued them together as a repair. The door beams can rot and leave the fibreglass panel all by itself, waving in the breeze. The door will drop and may move from top to bottom if this has happened, but it must be said this is an extreme state and we have only seen it this bad a couple of times.

The door cards (interior panels) can come adrift from the door structure as they are held in place by the door handle fixing, comprising three screws under the panel and two in the end of the panel. These screws go through the door card panel and into holes in the fibreglass of the door. If they have worked loose or fallen out it will require new self-tapping screws to secure it again, otherwise the door will become impossible to close properly, and if you slam it you risk damaging the door card panel. Keep an eye on this issue as it can be repetitive.

The Excel SE's rear, showing spats behind the wheels, the early boot spoiler and the SE badging.

The Excel door card featuring interior door handles, an ash tray and window and mirror controls.

Interior

This is definitely the weakest spot on the Excel and its companion models. Bits do tend to come off or become unstuck, but they are all generally easily fixed and re-stuck. The dash is normally sound and the switch gear is reliable and easy to use.

The mats can come adrift, but are easily fixed. Watch for wear of the leather seat pads, especially in rouche leather-trimmed cars, where high mileage can see the seams wear badly. The leather can be re-coloured and rejuvenated with a re-connolising kit, costing about £30 to £40, and a bit of care and elbow work. Gliptone Leather are the people to go to if you think you need to attempt this yourself. They have 'how to' videos on the internet and it isn't as hard as you think.

The interior did not change too much in the entire production run.

The ruched leather interior of later Excel SEs. Note the original gear knob.

The Celebration Excel interior with perforated leather, a coloured steering wheel and non-standard gear knob!

Headlining is very fragile and tends to wear inside the rear window where the sun dries it out until it splits. It can also just come away and hang down, ruining the interior. It can be repaired or replaced reasonably easily by those who know how.

Electrics

Door mirrors seem to have worked well throughout the model's history, the later ones being slightly better. Window motors can eventually give up the ghost, but this can simply require dis-assembly and lubrication, or attention to the bushes. The motors are not expensive to replace. The mechanism is bare steel and can be prone to corrosion damage, so check the joints and keep them greased up.

The main relays for the lights and the like are under the driver's side of the dashboard. If the grommet that allows the throttle cable through the bulkhead has been disturbed and not returned properly, or has come loose, water dripping from the hole will splash onto the relays and cause all sorts of electrical mayhem that seems random. Check it out.

Unlike the earlier Eclats and Elites, the headlamps are raised by motors, and these are very reliable in comparison to the vacuum system. There are very few problems with the Excel's electrics, thanks to Toyota parts and Lotus development work.

Wheels and Tyres

Other than kerbing the car there are no inherent problems with these items. New OZ wheels can be had for about £150 to £170 each and the earlier items are also available regularly at parts fairs, the Toyota items on the early Excels being relatively cheap and easier to find.

The original Goodyear Eagle tyres for the SE size (215 x 50 x 15) are unavailable, although there are excellent replacements available, just not in that size. You can either go down to 205 x 50 x 15 tyres – as on the normal model Excel, and this is the preferred choice for some Excel die-hards – or you can go up to the slightly wider 225 x 50 x 15s from makers like Toyo. I personally prefer these tyres and have found them to be excellent on the road, adding a little weight to the steering but also more feel and grip at the extremis. If you do go for the wider option you will need to be careful when steering on full-lock and reversing, as the extra width can cause the tyre to rub on the wheel arch slightly.

Be careful to check the age and condition of the tyres on the car when buying. Modern tyres have a shelf life of about six to eight, or possibly even ten years, if they are used regularly and looked after. However, even if they have done very few miles the rubber degrades and they become harder (like old cheddar) and subsequently less flexible. So,

The later Route OZ alloys with the wider than standard 225 x 50 x 15s fitted.

at every revolution of the tyre, the deformation and expansion as the tread meets the road leads to cracks and fractures, which may be hidden inside the tyre. This will lead to weakness where the tread is welded to the carcass of the tyre and the first you may know about this degradation is when you take your new toy for a spirited excursion and the tread parts company with the tyre with disastrous effect. It could be the end of both of you.

Checking the age of the tyre starts with the DOT code on the side of the tyre. If the code is only three digits long then the tyre is far too old (originating before 2000). If it has four digits you can read the date the tyre was manufactured in the following manner: the first two digits refer to the week number of the year it was made and the second two digits refer to the year. So, for example, 3610 would mean the thirty-sixth week of 2010.

The age of the tyres should not unduly affect your decision to actually buy the car but it should be a bargaining point, and certainly a safety point.

Exhaust

The late Excel SE pipe is wider bore than earlier systems but they all look very similar, with a cast manifold taking the four outlets into two ready for the start of the downpipe. The downpipe has a flexible steel joint where it begins under the car and leads into the large main silencer slung under the centre of the chassis. Behind the main silencer the pipe goes through a 'Y' splitter and snakes over and through the rear suspension and driveshafts. There are two rear silencers slung beneath the boot. I bought a stainless system from a Lotus main dealer and used the car every day for nearly five years, and about 60,000 miles, until the system failed. The weak spot is the flexible stainless steel joint on the downpipe, which can sever at either end on some systems and can be the first part of the entire system to give trouble. It can be re-welded by the right person as the heat in this section of the pipe tends to keep corrosion at bay.

On little-used cars the other main problem is the rear silencers and their connection to the rest of the system. The corrosive results of combustion don't get adequately vaporised and therefore sit in the system, where they condense. Have a good look for pin-holes in the pipes round the rear suspension, the 'Y' splitter and the silencers.

Miscellaneous

There can be problems with the throttle cable, wherein the pedal end ball can become detached, rendering the entire car immobile. It happened twice on my own Excel. Fortunately, it is not a difficult job to replace it.

The radiator is vulnerable due to its position at the front and down low. I managed to hole it three times in seven years. You don't need to go to the expense of total replacement; simply take the radiator to a refurbisher and pay about £100 to £150 for a full re-build, with a guarantee.

The clutch is Toyota but has AP Racing driven plates in it and is not cheap to replace. Mine had a hard start to life and still managed 50,000 miles. It's an 'engine out' job so don't buy someone else's problems.

Keep an eye on the rubber 'F' pipes on the top of the carbs. These can perish and split without seeming to have any marks on them and they adversely affect performance and fuel consumption.

4

Lotus Evora

Model History

The Evora was developed as Project Eagle at Lotus, culminating in the launch at the British International Motor Show in July 2008. The name was eventually decided upon by combining the words evolution, vogue and aura. Lotus were keen for all to know that they had developed the car in only eighteen months but it has a striking resemblance to the M250 prototype, especially from the front.

The Evora was the first new Lotus model since the launch of the Elise in 1995 to have a new chassis. There were three models expected to use the Evora platform but these have yet to emerge from Lotus. The platform is a larger aluminium extruded and bonded chassis tub with front and rear structures to carry the composite body and engine components. Mike and I went to Donnington Lotus Fair in 2008 and saw the two prototype Evoras on the Group Lotus stand. I will admit that at first sight I was not exactly enamoured. There was a white and a black example on view and they were roped off. There was also an Evora crash test mule that had the front clamshell removed to show how the crash structure had deformed after a series of crashes and how 'repairable' the new Evora was. It was clear to see how the front crash structure had deformed, crumpling the front prongerons in order to protect the rest of the chassis structure. What it also displayed was the evident quality of engineering and manufacture in the new chassis and suspension units. Lotus had certainly moved forward from the components on the Excels and indeed the Elise.

Mike and I wandered onto the stand, took some photographs, chatted with those around the cars and had a sit in the black Evora. We did wonder why everyone wasn't queuing to get a look but we took our time and eventually headed back to the entrance to the stand to leave, which now, strangely, had a rope across it. We were then lightly chided by a Lotus employee, who explained that the public weren't allowed in to see the cars up close! We apologised and I promised to buy one to make up for our faux pas. I stood by my promise, much later, but not in white or black!

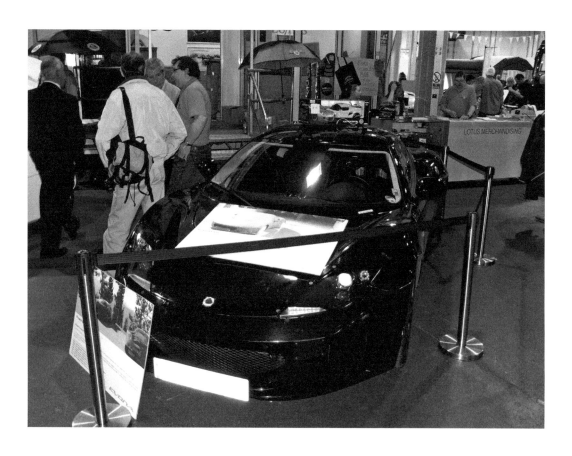

Above: The Evora prototype test car at Donnington in 2009.

Left: Evora prototypes at Donnington showing crash deformation.

The Evora crash structure, showing its ability to absorb heavy impact.

Evora prototype interior with a black centre console and the steering wheel that became brushed metal.

Sales of the Evora started with the launch model, the first 450 cars being offered with the 'Sport Pack', the 'Tech Pack' and the 'Premium Pack' already specified on the car. Although these cars were supposed to have a plaque on the dash to signify their launch status, my Evora does not have one. The rear bench seat was offered in the original Evora, hence its inclusion in this book. It was almost unique in being a mid-engined 2+2 vehicle at its launch, with only the BMW i8 claiming the same configuration.

The car cost £48,450 for the most basic Evora, with the 2+2 costing £2,375 more. The 'Sport Pack' gave the Evora a button on the dash that sharpens up the throttle response and allows a temporary extra 500 rpm before the rev-limiter cuts in. The intrusion of the traction control is also altered to allow greater yaw and slip before intervention. There is also a sportier diffuser at the rear and cross-drilled brake discs, with an oil cooler for the engine. If ticked as an option this was a bargain at £950 as it transforms the base car. Using the 'Sport' button changes the character of the car from sporty to very sharp and capable, especially in the throttle response department.

The 'Tech Pack' upgraded the Alpine stereo to a unit with a 7-inch touchscreen display that also has a satellite navigation unit built in and includes a 150 watt subwoofer in the rear, behind the driver. This unit also has built-in Bluetooth connectivity, allowing hands-free phone use. It is not the easiest unit to use every day, but as a small manufacturer Lotus does not have the millions required to create a bespoke unit. Also part of the pack was cruise control, operated from the steering wheel, rear parking sensors and a reversing

The original Evora design is a classic!

The back seats; I have never managed to get in the back of an Evora, but that doesn't mean it's impossible.

Switches to the right of the wheel are very stylish and work well – note the 'Sport' button!

camera that utilises the display in the Alpine stereo. There are also tyre pressure monitors, whose output is displayed on the main instrument binnacle in the small right-hand pane. This option was an extra £2,495 on the base car.

The 'Premium Pack' specified full leather interior trim for £2,495. The Evora was *Evo Magazine*'s Car of the Year in 2009.

At this point it should be explained that Dany Bahar, Lotus Chief Executive at the time the Evora was put into production, decided to announce Lotus' plans to introduce five brand-new models. These models included replacements for the Elan, the Elise, the Esprit, the Elite (four-seater) and a new larger car, the Eterne. There was no discussion of how this was to be funded, nor how the resources to achieve this monumental shift at Lotus were to be found. The Evora seemed to take a back seat at this time and we wondered where the publicity for this extremely capable and desirable car had disappeared to. Save one appearance of an early Evora on *Top Gear*, there did not appear to be a concerted publicity campaign from Lotus to sell the Evora.

The centre console has heating and ventilation controls, the entertainment system and switches for opening the glove box, among others.

The Evora interior is both comfortable and has a striking design.

Mirrors are care of Ford and Jaguar, as found on the X-Type.

Bahar eventually stepped down as CEO at Lotus after legal proceedings were abandoned by both DRB-Hicom (Lotus owners of the time) and Bahar, but in the meantime, in our opinion, the Evora did not receive the level of promotion it deserved as the first new Lotus model in many years. As mentioned, I saw one article on *Top Gear* that did not do the car justice, being one of Clarkson's pieces where the Evora was not really put through its paces like a similar Italian brand might have been. It did not even warrant a drive from the Stig! Like many enthusiasts, I did not see a great deal of press attention after the initial launch and was seriously disappointed by the lack of placement the Evora received. I was particularly gobsmacked and disappointed when *Top Gear* had a 'British Celebration' along the Mall in London and had JCBs, BMW Minis and an assortment of almost all the kit car manufacturers in the land, but there was not a single Lotus in sight!

Even now people ask me what my Evora is, and even if they know Lotus as a brand, they certainly have no recognition of the Evora as a model. Even my petrol-headed acquaintances comment on how brilliant the Evora looks in the ranks of Ferrari and Lamborghini for its presence and design touches, but wonder why they have not heard of its launch, let alone developments. A sad birth for such a brilliant car.

The engine is made more attractive with a lightweight cover.

The rear diffuser is not only good looking, it works well, leaving a lot of dust on the rear of the car.

Amazing space utilisation – the engine is squeezed in between the cabin and the small boot.

The Evora S

The Evora S was launched in 2010 to include larger wheels and a supercharger added to the 3.5 litre six-cylinder Toyota Camry engine. The supercharger is an Eaton TVS series unit and the installation was overseen by Harrop. This version of the Evora was available with an IPS (Intelligent Paddle Shift, by Aisin) option as a semi-automatic gearbox. The IPS versions of this model were slightly slower than the manual models but you will find that later IPS models are actually slightly quicker to 60, due to greater torque being supplied through the auto box. The wheels and tyres were uprated to Pirelli P Zero Corsa tyres on forged alloys, with 19-inch wheels on the front and 20-inch wheels on the rear. The price at launch was £61,500.

Model Year 2012 Updates

Midway through the production of the Evora and Evora S, Lotus updated and facelifted both models. The launch for the updates was at the Frankfurt Motor Show. Some of the changes across the range included the fitting of the close-ratio gearbox, Bi-Xenon headlights and body coloured door handles (replacing the chrome items) as standard.

There were new paint colour options, a further developed gear linkage, gear lever design and its positioning to improve the feel and precision of gear changes – a source of grumbles about the original car. A new, less fiddly Pioneer stereo was fitted as part of the 'Tech Pack' and replaced the original Alpine unit. The interior was revised with a new 'Premium Sport' option and there were new colours for the interior materials. Lotus used more leather coverings on extra surfaces to improve the ambience of the interior, including a slightly redesigned steering wheel that was available in black rather than bare metal.

The Evora Sports Racer, with a black front splitter and side sills, cornering hard!

The seats were still the Recarro items but they had new stitching and piping to improve their look. There was also a new exhaust design to provide a more sporting exhaust sound.

The Evora Sport Racer

The Evora Sport Racer was launched in 2013 and was a top specification Evora S with a distinctive paint scheme that saw a choice of only red, white, blue or charcoal grey for the car, with the roof, the rear diffuser, front splitter and area below the doors painted black, changing the appearance of the car strikingly. The price rose to £65,900.

The Evora 400

The Evora development work going on at Lotus looked to increase performance and extract even more power from the Toyota engine. The Evora 400 was unveiled at the 2015 Geneva Motor Show. It boasted a reworking of the overall styling with a revised interior and front and rear clams. The front has a more brutal look, with much larger apertures for cooling through the radiators and a rear that is more angular and incorporates a diffuser and new spoiler to improve down force. The price increased to £72,000.

Above the waistline the 400 looks like the previous models.

The 400 has a more menacing look to it with its larger air intakes. Note the new mirrors incorporating indicators.

The rear is more angular and the wheels are larger.

The name 400 represents the new power output of 400 bhp, this being achieved by further development of the engine, including the addition of an Edelbrok intercooler for the supercharging and remapping of the engine management.

The Evora 410

The Evora 410 swiftly followed at the same Geneva Motor Show a year later in 2016. It features further engine tweaks to deliver 410 bhp with a similar increment in torque to 310 lb/ft. Owners of the 400 could have the remapping done to their cars at Lotus dealers and gain the extra power without the other changes to the car.

The Evora 430 – GT and Sport

The Evora 430GT and Evora 430 Sport were launched in 2017, as Lotus once again moved into supercar territory and associated pricing. Only sixty of each model are planned to be built and neither has the back seating in place, so really it shouldn't be part of this book, but what a beautiful car the 430 is. It takes the Evora, and Lotus, into true supercar territory for the first time since the demise of the Esprit. With a staggering 430 bhp from the Toyota unit and further tweaking of the weight through the generous use of carbon fibre panels and new suspension settings, the Evora 430 takes on the other major manufacturers of sports cars globally. The 430GT is the wilder of the two models with a raised rear spoiler reminiscent of early Grand Prix cars. New frontal design improves air flow and aids downforce, while also looking extremely purposeful and worthy of a spot on any petrol-head's bedroom wall. The air intakes now look sculpted, with carbon fibre air blades built in to guide the air flow away from the front wheels. The rear of the front wheel arches is curved inwards, again to guide the air flow away from the front wheels. This is a case of a lot of small touches that make a huge difference overall.

The engine cover on the Sport is red, in common with the later limited edition Esprit Sport 350s. The engine cover comprises carbon fibre louvres, to save weight, as in the other 400 models. The 430 Sport was created to appeal to those prospective buyers who did not want the more extrovert looks of the GT. Both cars can be tailored to individual taste with many options for the interior of the car – Alcantara being the fabric of choice in the cabin – and most of the accoutrements being developed from the 400 and 410.

The 430GT develops up to 250 kg of downforce thanks to aerodynamic developments and the Sport 100 kg, without the raised spoiler. As a result, the GT has a top speed of 190 mph and the Sport a top speed of 196 mph. There are, for example, ducts in the top of the front wings that vent the pressure built up by the front wheels at speed and large ducts behind the rear wheels doing the same job. All this makes the Evora 430 Sport the fastest road car that Lotus has ever produced. It may not be a 2+2 anymore, but certainly worthy of a mention, I think!

Specifications

Evora
Engine: 3.5 litre, twenty-four valve, V6 Toyota VVTI unit.
Power: 276 bhp at 6,400 rpm / 350 Nm (258 lb/ft) at 4,600 rpm.

Economy: 30 mpg extra urban.
Performance: 0–60 mph 4.8 secs; Max Speed 162 mph.
Weight: 27.22 cwt (Unladen).

Evora S
Engine: 3.5 litre, twenty-four valve, V6 Toyota VVTI unit + Eaton Supercharger.
Power: 345 bhp at 7,000 rpm / 400 Nm (295 lb/ft) at 4,500 rpm.
Economy: 28.7 mpg extra urban.
Performance: 0–60 mph 4.4 secs; Max Speed 172 mph.
Weight: 28.21 cwt (Unladen).

Evora 400
Engine: 3.5 litre, twenty-four valve, V6 Toyota VVTI unit + Eaton Supercharger + Edelbrock charge cooler.
Power: 400 bhp at 7,000 rpm / 410 Nm (302 lb/ft) at 4,500 rpm.
Economy: 28.7 mpg extra urban.
Performance: 0–60 mph 4.1 secs; Max Speed 186 mph.
Weight: 27.46 cwt (Unladen).

Evora 410
Engine: 3.5 litre, twenty-four valve, V6 Toyota VVTI unit + Eaton Supercharger + Edelbrock charge cooler.
Power: 410 bhp at 7,000 rpm / 420 Nm (310 lb/ft) at 4,500 rpm.
Economy: 28.7 mpg extra urban.
Performance: 0–60 mph 3.9 secs; Max Speed 190 mph.
Weight: 26.08 cwt (Unladen).

Evora 430GT Evora 430 Sport
Engine: 3.5 litre, 24 valve, V6 Toyota VVTI unit + Eaton Supercharger + Edelbrock charge cooler.
Power: 430 bhp / 440 Nm (325 lb/ft).
Performance: 0–60 mph 3.6 secs; Max Speed 196 mph (Sport).
Weight: GT: 24.76 cwt Dry, 25.57 cwt Unladen; Sport: 24.57 cwt Dry, 25.37 cwt Unladen.
345 bhp per ton.

Evora Buyer's Guide

Again, this is by no means a comprehensive list of things to look for in an Evora. Take the time to have a look at the Lotus Forums (https://www.thelotusforums.com/forums/forum/259-evora-chat/).

Problems with the Evora include the air conditioning system. This is not particularly effective when it is working and is likely to stop working without the dealers knowing how to fix it. Mine has never worked properly, despite being refilled twice. Then, one winter's evening I entered my garage to get a screwdriver and it smelt strongly of solvents. I thought a paint can must have exploded, though I couldn't work out how in the cold conditions. Checking the cover on the Evora I spotted a bleached area on its static indoor cover, above the left-hand rear vent above the engine. The entire contents of the air conditioning system had vented through this area. This has yet to be rectified as I suspect the joint on the top of the high-pressure hose from the air-con pump.

My car can also flatten the battery after only three days or three weeks depending on how it feels. I have no idea what is causing this problem and nor did Newcastle Lotus!

The gearbox selector mechanism originally caused problems getting down into second gear, especially when the car was hot. A Lotus recall to replace a clutch pipe that was affected by engine bay heat went some way to curing the problem, but it can sometimes still be 'notchy', especially in hot weather and especially when compared with later revised models, although this problem has improved with use.

Dashboards and leather coverings on early cars can lose their integrity, with the glue failing and the leather rippling. This even happened with only 4,800 miles on a car that had spent its life in the factory! The best you get from the factory is a free replacement dashboard that you fit at your own cost.

There may be niggles on some cars but it appears to be a mechanically well-built model and is gradually acquiring the status it deserves.

Driving the Evora

My Evora – 2009 Launch Model

My Evora has a strange history, being possibly the first Evora to have the close-ratio gearbox fitted for testing by Lotus, not to mention it was reputedly used in the making of the original advert for the Evora. The car spent the first four years of its life with Lotus and had 4,500 miles on the clock when I took delivery.

I had been searching for an Evora for nearly a year after realising that my acquisition of an Aston Martin DB7 Vantage was a wonderful mistake! I am a complete petrol-head, to the point that the sound of a Merlin engine is written into my soul. I have heard that amazing V12 sound before and ran out of the house to see the Battle of Britain Flight heading towards a display, following the A1 north for easy navigation. That is how attuned I am! I had therefore bought and read the book *The V12 Engine* by Karl E. Ludvigsen and decided I needed to own a true V12-powered car before I died – hence why I became the owner of an Aston Martin DB7 Vantage. Three years and a lot of petrol money later, I started looking at the Evora.

I drove an Evora at Newcastle Lotus – a stunning yellow car with black leather – and was convinced immediately! I have driven DB9s and Ferraris, including the 360 Modena and contemporary models, but the Evora was a revelation. It felt lighter than almost all of these contemporary models and marques and almost danced along the road. It was more comfortable than my Jaguar daily driver and faster than anything else I had driven on a 'real' road.

A track experience in the Ferrari 360 Modena with the owner in the front seat was an eye-opener! The dash jumped up and down by nearly 2 inches as we went down the straight – a flat tarmac strip! He asked what I drove normally and when I told him I had an Elise he told me not to worry about the normal rules and to enjoy myself as he relaxed in the passenger seat. The 360 simply drove and felt like a big Elise with a nice engine note. There was no more explosive acceleration than in my Elise Sport 160 and the Elise felt more in direct contact with the road, while the go-kart feeling of an Elise, like you are wearing the car, is dulled in the Ferrari. The owner explained that he attended these experience days to subsidise his racing career but that the Ferrari was quite unreliable and costly to keep and that it was easy to see why they needed to be serviced every six months or 6,000 miles at exorbitant prices. Bear in mind that I know the owner of a 360 and he has paid out over £15,000 in the past six years just keeping it on the road, with even items such as the engine oil pump proving unreliable. The 360 drove well but was strangely uninspiring as it rattled and the interior tried to get outside of the cabin. It really did feel like a large Elise, but without the 'smile on your face' factor – the ache in the wallet helping to remove that, I would imagine. I didn't leave the experience searching the adverts for a Ferrari!

The yellow Evora was quite a different prospect altogether. From the first mile of driving it felt right. On the road it was so alive with feeling from the tarmac and with the 'Sport' button depressed it was extremely quick and involving. The brakes could crush your ribcage against the seatbelts and the suspension absorbed everything so well, yet produced amazing handling and no roll to speak of. It was the most responsive, dynamic and 'grown-up' Lotus I had ever driven. It even had the edge on the V8 Esprit I had driven, being more involving, with the same Lotus focus on the driving experience. As I said, I am lucky enough to own an Elise S1 Sport 160 and love the way it handles and accelerates like a playful beast, but the Evora takes this feeling to a more adult and sophisticated level. It was a real breath of fresh air!

The acceleration is in the same league as the Aston and Ferrari, being 4.9 seconds from 0 to 60 mph, and the sound of the original Evora was sporty but really quite restrained. The sharpened throttle response when the 'Sport' button was used turned the car into a much more keen and focused prospect. I could hurtle along the rural roads and brake hard enough to hurt my ribs without any complaint or fade from the braking system, and turn into a bend with total feel and confidence with no signs of under or oversteering. I could blast out of the corner with such precision the car felt like it was choosing the line itself and sticking itself to the tarmac. Trying the next and the next corner faster and faster on entry, steering gently and tightening the line at will while being amazed at the balance of the car, before tapping the power as soon as possible. My rowdiest behaviour couldn't unsettle the sublime balance of the chassis and power delivery. I had to have one and this was the one! Having had the car since 2013 and driven it on some excellent routes around the north-east Dales, I never fail to be amazed by its unflappable, capable and precise nature and by how it rewards all who take the wheel. The Evora's master card is its ability on substandard road surfaces and in weather conditions that render some supercars useless.

The view from behind the wheel; the original dashboard is prone to reflections.

Having driven the Evora and compared the cars that were for sale at the time, I decided I wanted an Ardent Red car. The black hid so many of the styling features, white was just not a Lotus colour and the metallic choices looked too tame for the styling in my opinion. The yellow was very tempting, but I had made up my mind. I spent eight months searching the internet and getting nowhere. I had all but given up when I got in from work one April night and realised that Newcastle Lotus had advertised a red Evora without contacting me! I left them an email to this effect and went to work the next day. I got a phone call at 8.30 a.m. to explain that the car had arrived at 5.20 p.m. the previous day, on a transporter that was sent to collect an Evora S IPS that needed an update to its gearbox software. The Lotus employee that delivered the car explained that it had been used in the advert video for the Evora and had been kept at the factory as an exhibit and development car since that time. If Newcastle Lotus could sell the Evora before the transporter returned, they would make a tidy profit.

I went there at 2.30 p.m. and Mike met me – on time for a change! I drove the car on the same roads I had driven the yellow car and bought it on the spot! I really upset a V8 Vantage owner who was prepared to let his car go for a lot less than they could be bought anywhere else and to pay the remainder in cash, all to be a Lotus owner!

Having bought the car, it had to be returned to the factory to be 'prepared'. This must have only consisted of changing the registration of the chassis number to the plates on the car as the air conditioning didn't work and there were no extra stamps in the service book. It took five weeks to return to Newcastle.

I contacted Andy Graham (the After Sales Administrator and Archivist at Lotus) and found out little other than that the car may have been the first to receive the close-ratio gearbox and it was the fourteenth close-ratio gearbox they had received. He confirmed that it had been in the factory but he didn't know what publicity it had been used for. Andy will check the production records for any Lotus you may own. He will provide a certificate showing when the car was manufactured and left the factory and any other salient facts about the car concerned for a small fee! Go to: http://www.lotuscars.com/ownership/certificate-provenance.

When I checked the publicity articles and video to see if my Evora was involved I discovered it was not part of the press demonstrators originally released to the press at launch. However, what I did find was that a car that bore my car's registration in magazine articles was in fact a completely different car with different wheels and a cream leather interior. I still have no explanation for this discrepancy and will be seeking more information in the future.

Driving the Evora 400

A friend of mine and owner of many Elans, including Elan +2s, had tried the Lotus Exige and found it great for belting around a track in the summer, but not quite as much fun on normal roads, especially in the English winter, so instead he searched around and asked about the Evora. I sang its praises and on my next visit he was the proud owner of a brand-new £72,000 Evora 400. The 400 he bought was in a custom dark blue colour and was quite a sight! In my humble opinion the front of the car did not look as special as the original car, appearing more openly aggressive without enough consideration for the original lines of the car. The large rectangular holes are obviously required for cooling but they remove the finesse of the previous nose. The rear is slightly better, with its more angular lines and deliberately purposeful diffuser, but I still prefer the original's softer lines and more integrated, stylish look.

The interior is re-modeled and looks more like a mid-range saloon and thus somehow less impressive. The dials themselves are actually an improvement to my aging eyes, as the numbers are much larger and better looking, and although the side displays are still spoilt by reflections, they are more legible without my glasses (which I don't need for driving).

I was given the keys and told to enjoy a trip around the village, some of which was visible and all of which was audible from Martin's drive. I pootled down the rutted lane and out onto the glorious country roads around the village. The first thing I noticed was the tighter, firmer steering, which was still light enough but much more direct, with less

The Evora 400 interior with its revised seats, centre console styling and main buttons along the top of the central dashboard.

extraneous feedback from the road. It struck me as being very like an early Esprit in its feel and weight. Once I got to the twisty bits it showed absolute brilliance in its weighting and feel. It feels directly connected to the road and much more purposeful, like it is being pushed into the tarmac, with the delicacy of the original Evora, or an Excel. You steer with movements from your wrists; imperceptible movements that give the impression your thoughts are being read. It goes where you feel it should and it feels like an explosion couldn't part it from its beloved road. The removal of some of the feedback from the original Evora's steering suits the extra power delivery and gives the driver confidence in abundance and a yearning to wring more and more speed from the amazingly responsive and sonically enthralling engine – especially with the exhaust button on the dash selected!

The next massive improvement over the original car is the gear change. The gear knob is much better to start off with, a chunky spherical aluminium item that already feels more substantial as soon as you hold it. Then the actual gate is much tighter and precise. It feels solid and directly connected to the cogs, and very pleasurable to use. The entire driving experience in the 400 is breath-taking. The car feels neck-snappingly fast and like it is welded to the road.

Martin had heard my enthusiasm down the straight, past the open fields! He was strangely pleased that I had opened his pride and joy up, briefly, and that he had heard the howl of the exhaust from nearly a mile away! I can only wonder and dream about what the new 430GT is like to drive!

The Evora 400 dashboard; note the clearer numbering on the dials, the changes to the side displays and the centre mark on the steering wheel.

Information and Clubs

The Internet

First of all, a cautionary note about Lotus internet forums, as with all websites, social media and forums. There are participants who have never used a spanner but who have read all of the books and magazine articles, and possibly own the car, even if only in 1:18 scale, and have studied the workshop manual and parts list in minutiae. These are the BBEs, as Mike and I call them, the 'Back Bedroom Experts'! They are small in number but they sometimes make the most noise.

Most decent forums have moderators who remove erroneous and fanciful posts but Mike has had several marathon posting strings with individuals who clearly don't know a feeler gauge from a torque wrench! You have been warned!

Here is a selection of websites where we trust the content:

Lotus Excel Net (www.lotusexcel.net/phpbb/) – A really good site for everything Elite, Eclat and Excel-based. Their archives are comprehensive and a seriously impressive resource.

SELOC – South East Lotus Owners' Club (www.seloc.org/) – A good site if you prefer a 'club' feel. Events, membership discounts and a free to users forum, this site caters for all Lotus models but has interesting information and is extremely useful.

The Lotus Forums (www.thelotusforums.com/) – Another really good site with tons of information and resources.

Parts Manuals & Information (www.rdent.com/manuals/index.html) – Parts information and manuals for all of the models in this book are available on this site. This is really useful if you need instant viewing of a parts manual, or have not gone to the expense of purchasing said manuals! Alternatively there are many PDF versions of Lotus manuals available on the internet for a lot less than the cost of a paper version.

Mechanicals

QED (Quorn Engine Developments) (qedmotorsport.co.uk/) – Lotus experts. They provide next-day delivery and comprehensive expertise and knowledge of all Lotus engines.

Burton Power (www.burtonpower.com/) – Experts on Ford-derived parts and tuning parts and have been for many years. An excellent place to find twin-cam parts and replacements.

Lotus Bits (www.lotusbits.com/) – Lotus Bits have been around for a long while and supply very good second-hand and reconditioned parts for all of the modern range of Lotus cars. Good prices and they might have what others don't!

SJ Sportscars (www.sjsportscars.co.uk/index.php?mod=9) – A good range of parts and a website that works well; there is generally a photo of the part with a description. Keen enough prices and 'Steve's alternative' parts make this a good place to look.

Kelvedon (www.kelsport.net/) – Very knowledgeable and good prices. They prepare Lotuses for racing; say no more!

Eurocarb (www.dellorto.co.uk) – All of the parts, jets, trumpets, etc. for the Dellorto carburettors on all Lotus models. Usually the best prices as well.

Bodywork

This really is the expert discipline in Lotus terms. Not just any repairer is adept at fibreglass repairs, nor at preparing and painting fibreglass cars. Some regular coachworks won't entertain the idea of working on fibreglass as it produces a huge amount of dust that can contaminate the paint shop. This is when you need to use a specialist, or alternatively someone who works with plastic and fibreglass as part of their craft – car customisers, for example. Always ask to see examples of their work, especially examples that have stood the test of time. Expect a reasonable cost with good fibreglass repairs and painting.

Always monitor any paintwork you have had done for a while after the work has been completed. Badly prepared paintwork will develop blisters, or blebs, or even small splits in the paint coat. This is because of moisture leeching through the fibreglass from behind and through the badly prepared gel coat upon which the paint sits.

Insurance

Insurance is getting more difficult to find at reasonable cost. The smaller, cheaper, independent insurance specialists have become bigger, greedier concerns over the years, so shop around and compare quotes.

You need to know that classic policies are slightly different to standard car policies. There are several important facilities in a classic policy that you need to consider. Agreed Value is just what it sounds like; you agree the value of your car at the outset of your policy and in the unfortunate event of you writing the vehicle off during your ownership, there is no quibbling about how much your settlement will be for your loss.

Limited mileage policies allow you to specify a limit on your annual mileage that reduces the insurer's risk and therefore the premium charged. The least mileage is usually 1,500 miles, rising in 1,500 mile increments to about 5,000 miles at the most. You might find restricting your miles is very beneficial to your budget and 3,000 miles is quite a reasonable allowance on a second, cherished motor that you don't take out in inclement weather.

Some policies allow you the option of buying back your beloved, again in the event of a total insurance write-off. You may want to consider this option seriously, as most of the time what an insurance company considers an uneconomic repair is nothing of the sort if done by specialists rather than main dealers. If you can undertake some of the work yourself you could even end up with a tidy sum left after the repairs, which you can use to run your pride and joy for several more years.

Here is a head start on where to look for your cover:

Classicline (www.classiclineinsurance.co.uk/) – By far the cheapest insurance we have found for Lotus cars in general and for a long time. They do multiple car policies as well. Unlimited mileage, breakdown cover and agreed value on classic policies. Haven't had to claim yet though!

Footman James (www.footmanjames.co.uk/) – Used to be the best for Lotus, and might still be where you live. Worth trying, and you can get a quote online.

Adrian Flux (www.adrianflux.co.uk/classics/) – Very close on price and certainly plenty of experience in the classics field. Lots of types of insurance too. Give it a go.

Peter Best Insurance – Again worth a try but less competitive since it expanded as a company.

Heritage Insurance have joined the classic insurers but I have not found them to be competitive with my models.

Parts and Replacements

Tyres

Demon Tweeks (www.demon-tweeks.co.uk/) – Very good for performance tyres and in odd sizes, so a good place to look.

Black Circles (www.blackcircles.com/) – This is another place that stocks almost every size of tyre and is extremely keen on price.

Always check the recommended forums first for where they are currently finding the best tyres at the best prices, as limited runs of specialist tyres can sometimes become available. This is a great source of useful tyre information: www.carbibles.com/tyre_bible.html

Carpets

Coverdale (www.carcarpets.co.uk/) – Sets for the Elan +2 start below £200 and go up to nearly twice this price for the woollen 'luxury' range. They also have carpet sets for the Elite and Excel, but not for the Evora as yet. They have a great selection of colours to suit any interior and even the cheapest range on offer is very good quality and fit, and is easily fitted by anyone with the most basic of skills. They even offer contrasting piping on your carpets if you ask nicely! They do all of the related products as well, like sound-proofing felt and spray adhesives.

I have found that patternone_autostyle on EBay sell good quality car mat sets that you can customise for general colour and the colour of the trimming material. The mats in my Evora came from this source.

Leather Care/Restoration

Gliptone (www.liquidleather.com/) – This is an area where you can get staggering results just by taking some time to watch the tutorial videos on how to use their products that have been posted on YouTube, and spending several hours of hard and concentrated work on your interior. Even just using their Scuffmaster product will reinvigorate very tired, creased looking leather, but their re-colouring products will make your leather look like new from the factory! This really is an area where time and elbow grease show great rewards, without expert intervention or expense. Have a go!

Storing Your Classic

The Engine

If you know the engine is not going to be used for a considerable length of time, it is worth draining the coolant (this is applicable to any classic car you may own, but the Lotus 900 series engines have some aluminium parts in the cooling system that do not need to be in contact with water if they are not being used). There are now products available from Evans Waterless Coolants that are glycol-based and therefore do not have the corrosive effect upon the internals of the engine and associated tubing. I will be using this fluid when I put my +2S on the road as the water sitting in the water pump during prolonged storage has been cited as the reason for water pump failure, which is an expensive business in the +2S.

Take the spark plugs out and spray the insides of the cylinders with WD40, and drip a little 3-in-one in as well. The engine being canted over, there will only be a proportion of the piston that will remain bathed in oil, but it is better than a completely dry cylinder. Then put the plugs back in. Remember you have done this when you first come to start the engine again as there will be smoke as the oil burns off initially.

Battery

You will need a battery cut-off switch and a trickle charger. The expensive side of the trickle charger market is usually the likes of CTEK, which starts at about £45. These are electronic controlled devices that work very well and even have cold weather settings. However, in my experience the best value trickle chargers are made by Maypole and cost about £15. They do an excellent job for a third of the price of the high-end articles.

Just fit your cut-off switch to the end of the negative battery lead and you can leave the battery on the car. When you are not going to use the car for a while you simply unscrew the knob on the cut-out and it disconnects the battery. If you require security as well, on most of these switches you can unscrew the knob completely and take it with you, rendering the car immobile.

When you want to leave the battery on trickle charge, simply disconnect the battery from the car's electrical system with the cut-off and connect the trickle charger to the terminals on the battery. The trickle charger replicates the alternator in charging the battery, stopping the charge when it is fully charged and re-starting the charging when the battery charge drops away a little. Limit your trickle charging to a couple of days a week to keep your battery healthy.

DO NOT try to charge a flat battery with a trickle charger or you will need a new trickle charger, expensive or not! DO NOT connect a trickle charger to a battery that is still attached to the car's electricals or ... well, you get the idea.

Brakes

When you store the car, do not leave the handbrake on. The pads will be in contact with the discs and they will probably seize to the discs eventually. Do not put the car away for any length of time after washing the car; it will be clean for when you come back to it but it will help to seize the brake pads to the discs and possibly help to corrode the pistons in the callipers if any of the seals are leaking. Store the car only when it is dry and has been driven as the heat will dry the brakes out and driving allows the pads to move away from the discs. Try not to use the brakes to stop the car in the garage, as this will ensure a gap between the pads and the discs. Ideally, and if a longer period of storage is required, jack the car up and free off the pads from the discs with a lever, carefully. If you can, make sure the handbrake linkages and cable are well greased where they can be seen and where they require movement.

Tyres

Either jack the car up and keep it raised off the ground – the best way to do this is with axle stands on each corner, or other stabilising stands – or use shaped rubber pads under the tyres to stop flat spots. There are specifically contoured pads called Tyre Trainers that are available through retailers like Hamilton Classics. These follow the curve of the tyre and spread the weight of the car away from the contact patch to maintain the shape of the tyre. This is a much better option than taking your pride and joy out of the garage in the spring and finding that you are driving on what feel like hexagonal tyres.

Interior

Silicon bags (Thomar AirDry Car Dehumidifier Set) are bags full of silica crystals that attract and absorb water vapour, like the ones found in electrical packaging. Place them near the windscreens and centrally in the cabin. They will absorb moisture that condenses on the cold of the windscreens. Use generous amounts of leather care cream before the winter – dry out the interior with the heater or hot air blower before storing and check on a regular basis.

Car Storage Covers and Cells

There are an extensive range of covers that are tailored to the shape of your Lotus, everything from light interior covers that are primarily to protect the bodywork from splashes and dust to heavy, multi-layered covers that are for outdoor use and protect against the effects of the sun on the paintwork and the environment upon the car as a whole. One of the primary threats to all classics when they are outside is bird strike! Bird poo eats paintwork and blisters the layers of paint if not removed as soon as humanly possible. I have experience of the lengths these avian critters will go to get at your Lotus – the crows this year decided that they would eat my expensive new cover and take strips away to line their nests! Next-door's cat also decided to sharpen its claws on the front of my Excel cover! There are prices to suit every pocket in the cover market, so shop carefully. Hamilton Classics have an extensive range and have been very reasonable when there have been problems with a cover.

Car cells are expensive and, for me at least, are not proven to improve protection at all. Unless you use your garage for other things that are likely to constantly cover your beloved in harmful particles, a good lined interior cover will do the job as well. I am sure that my 'Carcoon' simply kept the moisture in the air inside the cell and circulated it around the car more efficiently! The rust positively blossomed. It did stop a disintegrating garage roof from damaging the car, however, so decide if you really need that level of protection before you make the leap. They are also a bind if you want to use the car regularly as deflating, unzipping and getting the car out is a cumbersome process that needs to be reversed when you put the car away again.

Epilogue

This trek through Lotus' more practical models started with the marque expanding its world-beating Elan sports car to accommodate more seats and luggage to produce a beautiful and capable coupé and ends with the complete opposite, with the back seats being removed from the Evora to turn it into the fastest two-seater road car Lotus has ever produced.

I hope this meander through Lotus' 2+2 offerings has whetted your appetite for the marque and the models featured. If you want to know what the much talked about 'Lotus' DNA' means, watch the *Project M50* documentary and listen to Colin Chapman in the twenty-fifth minute of the programme as he espouses, as only he could, what values make a Lotus road car like no other.

So now having absorbed and pondered, go and drive, as nothing explains what Lotus really stands for like driving one.